SHENANDOAH
COUNTY
IN THE
CIVIL WAR

SHENANDOAH COUNTY
IN THE
CIVIL WAR

FOUR DARK YEARS

HAL F. SHARPE

THE
History
PRESS

Published by The History Press
Charleston, SC 29403
www.historypress.net

Copyright © 2012 by Hal F. Sharpe
All rights reserved

Cover art: "The Lions of the Hour: The VMI Cadets at the Battle of New Market." *Courtesy of Keith Rocco, www.keithrocco.com.*

First published 2012

Manufactured in the United States

ISBN 978.1.59629.760.9

Library of Congress CIP data applied for.

Contents

Introduction

In 1860, the economic fortunes of Shenandoah County looked very bright. The drought of the two previous years had dissipated, and the wheat crop was abundant. A new rail line, the Manassas Gap Railroad, connecting the port of Alexandria with most of the towns of the county, brought the promise of increased trade with Europe. The county's rich beds of iron ore were being processed in iron furnaces scattered throughout the county. One of the best macadamized roads in the nation, the Valley Pike, ran through the heart of the county, providing an all-weather route for stagecoaches and freight wagons hauling passengers and trade goods for a prosperous people. Herds of fine cattle and sheep were driven to market along Ox Road. Despite the ominous political clouds on the horizon regarding the future of slavery, the future looked very promising.

In less than one year, however, fortune would reverse itself. Those ominous clouds of the previous decade burst forth into a hurricane of death and destruction: the American Civil War. At 4:30 a.m. on April 12, 1861, Confederate artillerists in Charleston Harbor fired a ten-inch mortar shell that burst over the Federal garrison at Fort Sumter, signaling the beginning of the Civil War. That single incident more than five hundred miles away changed the lives of the people of Shenandoah County in ways they never could have imagined.

In 1860, the population of the county stood at 13,896, including 753 slaves. The county had no large or strategically important cities and no prominent war industries, and it trailed by a small measure its neighboring counties in agricultural production. Its geographic location, in the center of the Shenandoah Valley surrounded to the east and west by mountains, made it impractical as base for extensive enemy military operations.

Yet by the end of the war, there was scarcely a mile along the Valley Pike in Shenandoah County where fighting did not take place. The county was the scene of four significant battles: New Market, Tom's Brook, Fisher's Hill and part of Cedar Creek. The Battle of New Market is one of the more storied battles of the war, primarily because of the heroic charge made by the cadets of the Virginia Military Institute. The horrifically bloody Battle of Cedar Creek marked the end of Confederate control in the Shenandoah Valley.

So how did that first shot in Charleston Harbor, more than five hundred miles from Shenandoah County, alter the lives and fortunes of Shenandoah County citizens? This book, in a small way, attempts to answer that question.

1

Shenandoah County

A Land of Milk and Honey

S henandoah County is located in the heart of the scenic Shenandoah Valley of Virginia. The county is bounded by Frederick County in the north, Rockingham and Page Counties in the south, Page and Warren Counties in the east and Hardy County, West Virginia, in the west. Cedar Creek marks the boundary between Frederick County and Shenandoah County. Surrounded on the east and west by mountain ranges, the central plain of the county is a series of rolling fields and rich farmland intersected by the North Fork of the Shenandoah River and a number of flowing creeks that provide moisture for the fields and power for a variety of mills along their banks.

The Massanutten Mountain is the most significant topographical feature in Shenandoah County, dominating the landscape on the eastern side of the county. The Massanutten is actually a series of steep ridges that bisect the Shenandoah Valley just east of Strasburg in the north and stretch south for about fifty miles to the highest peak east of Harrisonburg in Rockingham County. The mountain is divided into northern and southern sections, with the New Market Gap being the division point. The northern section consists of three roughly parallel ridges, forming two smaller valleys. The wider inner valley is called Fort Valley, while the smaller one is known as Little Fort Valley. The ridges of the northern section converge at New Market Gap.

Located at the northwestern terminus of the Massanutten is an imposing formation known locally as Signal Knob or, alternately, a part of Three-Top Mountain. Signal Knob was used throughout most of the war by one

Signal Knob was one of the most prominent locations in the county during the Civil War.

side or the other as an observation post and signal station to relay vital information on troop movements. Control of Signal Knob afforded the occupying force the ability to observe troop movements in large parts of three counties. The terrain of the Massanutten and Signal Knob is one reason some of the most significant battles of the valley's 1862 and 1864 campaigns occurred in this area.

A RURAL PARADISE

Even before the Civil War, the Shenandoah Valley was often described as a rural paradise. The valley was a peaceful place dotted with small towns and villages, well-kept homes, vast fields of grain and livestock and prosperous mills. Breathtaking views from New Market Gap, Rude's Hill, Fort Mountain and Signal Knob can hardly be surpassed. The rich fields of Meem's Bottoms, level and productive as an Illinois prairie, and other farming lands along the Shenandoah River and its tributaries have long been a subject

Fertile plains of Meem's Bottoms on the estate of Mount Airy. This ground was the scene of combat throughout much of the war.

of renown and pride. According to Champ Clark in *Decoying the Yanks*, one Confederate soldier said in 1861 that the rolling green valley "was truly a land of milk and honey." But that land of milk and honey would change dramatically over the next four years.

THE PEOPLE OF THE COUNTY

During the seventeenth century, pioneers, mostly of German ancestry, migrated from Pennsylvania along what was known as the "Great Wagon Road" and settled in Shenandoah County. Once here they become farmers, merchants, artisans and tradesmen. Villages sprang up every few miles along the way. The Germans were joined by Swiss and Scotch-Irish settlers, but Germans remained the dominant ethnic group. For the next one hundred years, the German language was still spoken in many county homes and churches. A German-language newspaper was published in New Market for a number of years. Religion was an important part of the culture, and most of the popular denominations were represented in the county. People of the Quaker, Dunkers and Mennonite faiths were part of the fabric of the county, but by 1860, most of the Mennonites had moved to Rockingham County. By the conclusion of the colonial period, the county's unique migration pattern had helped to create a cultural landscape in Shenandoah and the surrounding counties strikingly different in many ways from the established patterns of eastern Virginia. Small, privately owned farms, intensive grain and livestock agriculture, ethnic diversity and religious pluralism all contrasted sharply with the culture of tobacco production, plantation life, social stratification, Anglicanism and large slave populations that defined the commonwealth's long-settled Tidewater region.

While there was certainly a sizable upper strata of society in Shenandoah County, in terms of numbers, the majority of the county's residents were a mixture of modest farmers and part-time laborers. Their farms were smaller and usually located in rockier and less fertile soil than the richer bottomlands occupied by the larger landowners. In good harvest years, these small farmers could still produce crop and livestock surpluses that could be sold or bartered. The citizens of Shenandoah County of 1860 had many shared values that still exist today. Strong family ties, pride in their ancestors and a sense of community were prevalent throughout the county in 1860 as they are today.

THE ECONOMY

Prior to the Civil War, the economy of Shenandoah County depended heavily on agriculture. Thanks to an ample supply of water, rich limestone soil and a mild climate, the county was ideally suited for agriculture. Early in the nineteenth century, farmers grew large crops of flax, hemp, tobacco and varieties of grain, as well as raised livestock, which they were able to sell to eastern markets. Since hemp and tobacco required a great deal of manual labor, most of the local farmers turned to wheat as their cash crop because it needed less labor.

Shenandoah Valley farmers produced almost twenty bushels of wheat per capita, while farmers of the other nine growing regions of the state produced fewer than six bushels per capita. The great volume of grains produced here caused this region to be called the "Granary of the Confederacy" during the Civil War. Of course, these same circumstances led to the emergence of the

Ruins of the Alum Springs (Henrietta) Furnace near Orkney Springs.

valley as an important target for Federal armies seeking to destroy sources of supply for the Confederate army.

The majority of farms in the county were of moderate size, ranging from one hundred to three hundred acres. While wheat was the cash crop, livestock was also a vital part of county farm production. Cattle and hogs, raised in great numbers throughout the county, were driven to markets in Baltimore and Alexandria. Many farms also raised sheep primarily for the wool they produced.

Hams and bacon were cured in large quantities in area smokehouses. Sawmills became more plentiful and productive by using hired slave labor. The furnaces became a major source of pig iron for forges in Maryland and Pennsylvania. Manganese and zinc ores were also mined intermittently after 1834.

Wheat production, the dominant source of wealth in the valley, drove a host of other industries. Before the advent of McCormick's reaper, a good deal of labor was required to harvest the wheat. Once the wheat was harvested, it had to be hauled by wagon to mills where it was processed into flour. Coopers or barrel makers were needed to make the barrels into which

Whissen House, located in Edinburg. This house was the home of E.B. Whissen, owner of Whissen Mill at the time of the war.

the flour was placed. The flour was then hauled to market, at first by freight wagons along the Valley Pike and later by rail, where it was sold.

Business-savvy millers were important players in this system, often serving as the "middleman" between growers and buyers. It was often the millers who calculated the cost of capital, labor and transportation. Together with banks, they arranged for credit acceptable to both the producers and hauling services and made deals with East Coast markets and in some cases with European buyers. It was this access to distant markets that created a prosperous and stable economic and social order.

Many of the local manufacturing interests, which once met only the needs of local customers, expanded as better transportation gave them access to other markets. The late 1840 and '50s saw the advent of a number of manufacturing concerns in Shenandoah County. In 1848, the Mount Jackson Manufacturing Company began. In 1851, the Edinburg Manufacturing Company was chartered to produce woolen goods, flour and lumber, among other things. For many years, Strasburg and New Market were important centers for the production of pottery, decorative vases and jugs so important to local distillers. As the economy improved, so did their businesses. Colonel Levi Rinker operated a woolen mill, a carding mill and several other enterprises along Mill Creek just west of Mount Jackson. Local tanneries, distilleries and wagon-making facilities expanded their businesses and took on new employees, including some slaves.

Iron production, the county's primary manufacturing industry, was both a source of wealth and employment. Iron furnaces in the county in 1860 included Columbia Furnace, Liberty Furnace, Van Buren Furnace, Henrietta Furnace and Caroline Furnace. Surrounding each furnace was a host of companion facilities, such as hotels, stores, housing for employees and sometimes even a post office.

Tourism was beginning to flourish in Shenandoah County thanks to the publicity received from printed media touting the value of "tak[ing] the waters" in the county's famous spas at Orkney Springs and Seven Fountains.

2

Roads and Rails

The first settlers entering the valley from Maryland crossed the Potomac River by way of fords located at Williamsport, Shepherdstown and Harpers Ferry and then followed the Warrior Trace en route to a new life. Gradually, the route was improved to handle heavier wagon traffic, and the resultant route became part of the Great Wagon Road, which ran from Philadelphia across western Maryland, through the valley and into the Carolinas.

The growth of population and commerce in the valley created a pressing need for better transportation. The Great Wagon Road was still basically a dirt track filled with ruts and potholes. Rivers and creeks had to be crossed using fords in most cases, and in bad weather, the route was barely passable. Locals, as well as merchants in the East, pressed for a better road system. Accordingly, on March 3, 1834, the Virginia General Assembly passed legislation creating the Valley Turnpike Company, a public-private venture with the Virginia Board of Public Works, which held a 40 percent investment in the project. The original Valley Turnpike was to be sixty-eight miles long, running from Winchester to Harrisonburg. Three years later, another twenty-five miles were added to the pike through a merger with another corporation, which stretched the road to Staunton.

The company was allowed to use as much of the Great Wagon Road as was desirable, but the work was both difficult and time-consuming. The new construction had to share the right of way with existing traffic, and a great deal of grading was needed to make the new route suitable for

Sketch of the construction of the Valley Pike in the 1830s.

macadamizing. Macadamizing consists basically of compacted layers of small stones cemented into a hard surface by means of stone dust and water (water-bound macadam). Macadamizing required three layers of stones laid in a sloping manner from a crown in the center to ditches built on both sides of the road for drainage. The first two layers consisted of hand-broken aggregate laid to a total depth of about eight or nine inches. The third layer was approximately two inches thick with a maximum aggregate size of about one inch. The layers were compacted with a heavy roller, causing the angular stones to lock together.

The Valley Pike was built without the use of heavy mechanized earth-moving machinery, so most excavation was done by sweating men with picks and shovels. Labor to build the Valley Pike came from a variety of sources, including the local farmers (who worked on the road as part of their financial commitment to the project), slaves hired from their masters and day-laborers hired locally as needed.

The dimensions of the Valley Turnpike were about twenty-two feet wide with eighteen feet being paved. No grade was to exceed three degrees. Limestone was quarried along the route, thus altering the landscape through

18

Photograph of the Valley Pike as it looked in the 1880s. This was one of the finest roads in the country at the beginning of the Civil War.

which the road passed. The limestone was also used to line ditches and culverts through which water could be drained.

Tollhouses were set up about every five miles to collect toll monies, which were used for upkeep and other improvements to the road. The price of the toll for a five-mile stretch was five cents. At least one of the original tollgate houses still stands on the northwest corner of Main and North Streets in Woodstock. The Valley Turnpike quickly became the most important transportation route through the Shenandoah Valley. Other sections were quickly added so that by the time of the Civil War, the road extended from the Potomac River at Williamsport to Lexington. The pike became the centerpiece for an intricate web of roads throughout the valley. In most places, the modern network of state and county roads overlays the historic network.

Good serviceable bridges were an important part of the Valley Pike. Most of the pike bridges were covered to protect the bridge deck from the negative effects of weather. These old wooden bridges were masterpieces of architecture, usually built by local men such as John Woods and Robert Jones from Hawkinstown who were master bridge builders.

Cedar Creek Bridge as it looked in the 1890s.

During the war, most of the bridges were burned by one or the other of the contending armies to prevent their use by the enemy. Flimsy temporary replacements were built, but frequently the replacement bridges were also destroyed only to be rebuilt again. As a result of their frequent destruction, Federal armies in the valley often carried pontoon bridges as part of their train. The location of bridges at Cedar Creek, Narrow Passage, Edinburg and Mount Jackson were important both strategically and tactically. Beginning with the aftermath of the First Battle of Kernstown, combatants fought for possession of these bridges and even the crossings themselves dozens of times over the next three years.

The Valley Turnpike made the Shenandoah Valley a far easier place for armies to march than eastern Virginia or Maryland. There was little dust on the road, and troops were often able to march in the adjoining fields, where the soft turf was a great relief to weary feet and frequent groves shaded the columns from the direct sun. The supply of water was abundant, and the roads on which the wagon trains moved were generally excellent. The Valley Pike could accommodate two parallel columns of army wagons.

The army that controlled the Valley Pike had the advantage of being able to move swiftly up or down the valley, while its enemies were bogged down on the muddy side roads. Not surprisingly, most of the Shenandoah Valley's battles were fought somewhere along the Valley Turnpike.

At the time of the Civil War, Shenandoah County roads fell into three categories. The finest road was obviously the Valley Turnpike with its macadamized surface. Two other turnpikes built during this period were those that improved travel to Orkney Springs and through Fort Valley. On February 6, 1856, the Mount Jackson & Howard's Lick Turnpike Co. was incorporated. Howard's Lick and Orkney Springs, with their mineral springs, were becoming tourist attractions, so a good road was needed to serve the springs and the small villages along the route. About that same time, a charter was issued to the Powell's Fort Turnpike Company to construct a pike beginning at the Waterlick rail depot and running through the entire length of Powell's Fort Valley and over to the Valley Turnpike.

Other fairly good roads were known as a "grades," such as the Cedar Creek Grade. Grades were usually built with a crown in the center to aid with drainage. The third category of roads was simply called dirt roads. These roads were difficult to traverse during extended periods of bad weather. Many dirt roads were simply farm lanes, but others were important secondary roads that became strategically critical during the Civil War. Two important dirt roads that ran parallel to the Valley Pike through the county were the Back Road and the Middle Road. The Back Road, which skirted the flank of Little North Mountain, was mountainous and in many places difficult to travel, even during good weather. The Middle Road traced a meandering course between the Back Road and the Valley Turnpike. Since the Valley Pike's surface was hard on the hooves of cattle, most farmers used the Middle Road for moving their herds. As a consequence, it became known as "Ox Road."

The county roads and bridges were damaged and destroyed as the armies tramped back and forth and fought over them repeatedly. During the later stages of the Civil War, the Valley Turnpike Company reported that its revenue collections were negligible because "of the army destroying bridges, injuring toll houses, and we are getting very little tolls." Every bridge along the Valley Pike in Shenandoah County was severely damaged or destroyed during the war. Turnpike company officials argued that the cost of labor and supplies had risen exponentially during the war, so the company needed permission to increase tolls at least eightfold. The financially strapped Confederate government paid only one-quarter of the tolls the company was entitled to collect. Transporting the heavy rail equipment along the Valley Pike left deep gouges in the surface that were never adequately repaired until after the war. Somehow, the Valley Turnpike Company managed to recover sufficiently from the rages of war to remain in operation into the early twentieth century.

In 1918, the Valley Pike was incorporated into the state highway system. Designated initially as State Route 3, the designation was changed to State

Route 11 in 1926. The Valley Pike has remained the principal local north–south thoroughfare within the county for more than 150 years. Today's road network follows the original routes to a great degree, making it easy to trace the paths of history through the county. As several authors have said, "Route 11 is like a history book, each chapter overlaying the other."

THE MANASSAS GAP RAILROAD

The Manassas Gap Railroad (MGRR) was chartered in 1850 to connect eastern markets and the Port of Alexandria with the agriculturally rich Shenandoah Valley. The original plan called for the railroad to be built incrementally from its connection with the Orange and Alexandria Railroad (O&A) at Manassas Junction to Harrisonburg in Rockingham County. With financial assistance from the Virginia Board of Public Works, construction began in 1851. The line ran west through Manassas Gap, which gave the line its name, reaching Strasburg by 1854. From Strasburg, the line turned south, reaching Woodstock in 1856 and Mount Jackson by 1859.

The president of the MGRR was Edward C. Marshall, son of famed chief justice John Marshall. A number of prominent Shenandoah County citizens owned stock in the MGRR, including Gilbert S. Meem, George Hupp, George Grandstaff, Israel Rinker, Andrew and Philip Pittman, Mark Bird, Jacob Lantz and Israel Allen. Dr. Andrew Meem served on the board of directors for a number of years.

During the summer of 1861, the Manassas Gap Railroad became the first railroad in history to move troops directly to an ongoing battle when Confederate forces from the Shenandoah Valley were transported to Manassas Junction during the Battle of First Manassas.

The route of the railroad through Shenandoah County generally followed the Valley Turnpike from Strasburg to Mount Jackson, and stations were built along the way in every town except Tom's Brook and Maurertown. Extensive rail equipment maintenance facilities were built in Woodstock. From Mount Jackson, plans called for the railroad to go southwest to Forestville and Broadway before going on to Harrisonburg.

It might seem odd that a railroad destined for Harrisonburg would go through Forestville instead of following the Valley Pike along a more direct route, but politics came into play. Business interests such as stage lines and freight companies, as well as certain Valley Turnpike Company officials, thought the railroad would hurt their businesses, and they found allies in the town of New Market. Several influential citizens of New Market objected to the railroad coming through New Market because the noise of the railroad engines would "frighten the milch [*sic*] cows and grazing steers."

The MGRR was built in sections, each one contracted to a professional railroad builder. With the railroad complete to Mount Jackson, the next section to be built was to run from Mount Jackson to Harrisonburg. The contract for this section was awarded to Michael Graham, a native of Ireland who had come south from Pennsylvania with his wife, Catherine, and two small children. Little is known about Graham until 1860, when he showed up at Mount Jackson. Graham purchased the Central Hotel and a fine brick home in Mount Jackson.

Graham hired about ninety men, mostly Irish immigrants, to begin the construction of the new section of the railroad. By April, the roadbed had been graded as far as Forestville, and the railroad trestles were partially completed. The rails for this section, purchased by the MGRR in England, had been delivered and were stored in Alexandria awaiting transport to the valley. The advent of war stopped construction completely, and it was not resumed until after the war.

When construction stopped, Graham began gathering hay and buying horses for the Confederacy in order to avoid being drafted into the Confederate army. He may have provided the lumber to build the Confederate Hospital at Mount Jackson. Many of his Irish laborers joined the Southern army, becoming the nucleus of the Emerald Guard, a company in the Thirty-third Virginia Infantry. Graham tried to discourage his men from enlisting and as a result came under suspicion of being a Union sympathizer. In April 1862, when Federal army major general Nathaniel Banks first entered Mount Jackson, Graham offered Banks his services. When Major General John C. Frémont occupied Mount Jackson following the battles at Cross Keys and Port Republic, Graham provided him with a great deal of supplies. Frémont took over Graham's hotel and turned it into a temporary hospital. When Frémont left Mount Jackson, Graham went along, leaving his wife and children alone in Mount Jackson. Mrs. Graham was placed under what we call today "house arrest." When local officials learned that Michael Graham was scouting for the Federals, Mrs. Graham was formally arrested and sent first to Harrisonburg and then to Richmond for an unknown period of time.

This was not the end of the Catherine Graham story by any means. Among the documents recovered from General Robert Milroy's office following the Battle of Second Winchester was a report dated February 15, 1863, from

Michael Graham to Major General H.W. Halleck concerning observations made by his wife, Catherine Graham, "whilst traveling as a spy from Mt. Jackson up the Valley to Staunton, thence to Richmond, and thence, by way of Culpeper, Woodville, Sperryville, Little Washington to Piedmont, thence to New Berlin, on the Baltimore and Ohio R.R., thence to Washington city." She says that from Culpeper she rode as far as Baltimore in company with Mrs. Kelley, of Staunton, and Mrs. Kennedy, of Culpeper, whom she thought, "from their actions and conversation, were two rebel spies."

Part of Graham's report subsequently appeared in the *Official Records of the Civil War* and reads as follows:

> *My wife, Catherine Graham, who left Mount Jackson, Shenandoah County, Virginia, some three weeks since, having arrived here on last Wednesday, gives me the following account of their strength, &c., in the region of country which she has passed through. She went from Mount Jackson to New Market, where General Jones' command is, consisting in part of three regiments of infantry, two batteries of artillery and a battalion of cavalry. When she left Mount Jackson, there was but a guard to regulate the hospitals. Imboden has command of the cavalry at Harrisonburg; there are not more than 30 men. When General Milroy's cavalry went up to Woodstock, they removed the deposits of banks in Rockingham and Staunton to Lynchburg. At that time a regiment of cavalry could have captured Staunton without meeting any resistance. There were 800 sick in hospital at Mount Jackson; there had been sixteen cases of small-pox amongst them. Major [Alexander] Baker has charge of the hospitals; he is a relative of Ashby.*

Michael Graham worked throughout the rest of the war for various Union generals, including Banks, Frémont, Hunter and Meade, sometimes being known as a "confidential agent" and other times as a scout or detective. Graham provided information on Confederate movements and successfully arrested a Jewish blockade runner at Martinsburg. After the war ended, Graham and his family returned to Mount Jackson. In 1871, Graham filed at least two claims with the Southern Claims Commission. In one of the claims, he requested and received almost $4,000 in compensation for the lumber and bricks used to build the Confederate hospital. In his claim, Graham did not mention the Confederate hospital, choosing instead to claim that the buildings in question were actually farm buildings and stables on his property. After the war, the Federals dismantled the hospital and took the building materials to Rude's Hill, where they built their occupation camp. Interestingly enough, the government paid his claim.

Returning to the MGRR during the war, the company hired bridge guards to prevent sabotage in 1861. In May, two railroad guards named Holtzman and Coffee were run over and killed by a locomotive on the bridge in Edinburg. According to a Richmond newspaper, "From the fact that a lot of straw was found near the bodies, it is inferred that the men had laid down on the bridge for a nap, and did not awake until the train was too near for them to escape. The bodies were dreadfully mangled."

THE GREAT TRAIN RAID OF 1861

Strasburg and the MGRR played a major role in the most spectacular raid on a railroad in the Civil War. In 1861, the main east–west line of the Baltimore and Ohio Railroad (B&O) crossed the Potomac River at Harpers Ferry. When Virginia Militia troops seized the partially destroyed U.S. arsenal located there, they also came into control of a portion of the B&O mainline. On May 23, Virginia closed the railroad and captured a great deal of railroad rolling stock and equipment. The following day, Major General Joseph E. Johnston assumed command of all the troops at Harpers Ferry and immediately began preparations to withdraw closer to Winchester. Johnston, after coordinating with Richmond, began his withdrawal and ordered Jackson to destroy as much B&O equipment and track as possible. Jackson's troops, together with the militia, began the destruction on May 25.

The South needed railroad equipment, especially locomotives, so a bold plan was concocted to save at least part of the equipment. Captain Thomas R. Sharp and a group of experienced railroad men were sent to Martinsburg to select and remove locomotives, rail cars and equipment that was not too badly damaged to be useful on southern railroads. Over the next several months, at least fourteen locomotives and tons of equipment was removed and carried overland to Strasburg for use by the South.

A few small engines were moved by rail from the B&O to Winchester using the tracks that belonged to the Winchester & Potomac Railroad (W&P), but the Confederates mistakenly burned the bridge over the Opequon Creek, effectively blocking that line. With the bridge over Opequon Creek destroyed, each locomotive chosen for removal had to be hauled more than seventy miles over the Valley Pike before reaching Strasburg. Many of the

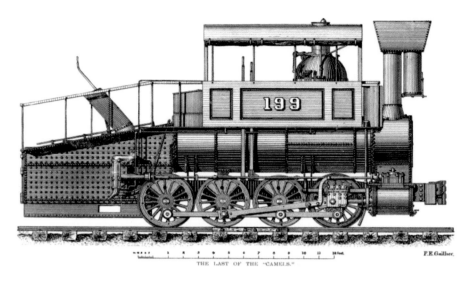

THE LAST OF THE "CAMELS."

P.E.Gailher

Sketch of Baltimore and Ohio engine #199, which was hauled overland from Mount Jackson to Staunton.

rail cars that had been captured were hidden in barns and farms throughout the Winchester area. B&O equipment continued to be moved south through the summer months of 1861 and even for a period of the next two years. By July 25, Sharp reported that eighty cars had been successfully moved onto Confederate rails.

To move the massive locomotives, the tender was uncoupled and then the engine was raised by means of jackscrews and stripped of all the parts that could be removed. All the wheels were removed except the large flange drivers at the rear. The engine was then hoisted into the air, and the missing forward wheels were replaced by a heavy truck made of iron-shod wooden wheels. When the jacks were removed, the engine rested on the flange drivers and the wheels of the new truck. A crew of men went ahead of the engine to strengthen the bridges. A newspaper report from Strasburg on September 7, 1861, stated, "Fourteen locomotives, a large number of railroad cars, nine miles of track, telegraph wires and about $40,000.00 worth of machinists' tools and materials, all belonging to the B&O Railroad, have been successfully hauled overland by the Confederates."

The last of the captured locomotives to be taken to Richmond was engine #199. The engine had already been hauled to Strasburg and was ready to be conveyed to Richmond when Johnston evacuated his positions around Manassas, cutting off the eastern connection between the MGRR with the Orange and Alexandria (O&A) Railroad. No longer could the captured B&O engines be sent to Richmond by this route. To get the #199 to Richmond, it was taken by rail to Mount Jackson, removed from the rails and hauled seventy miles over the Valley Pike to Staunton, where it was again placed on the rails of the Virginia Central and hauled to Richmond. The trip from Mount Jackson took about four hurried and exciting days. Once again, many bridges had to be strengthened en route, and in some cases, the horses had to be unhitched to lighten the load on the bridge. The engine was then moved across the bridge by means of a block and tackle. The engine turned over en route, only adding to the turmoil required to move the beast. When it arrived in Staunton early in the morning, the major portion of the population was up and out to see the novel cavalcade.

When General Banks captured Mount Jackson on April 17, 1862, he reported the seizure of two other locomotives and several railroad cars. On May 23, 1862, Colonel Turner Ashby's Seventh Virginia Cavalry tore up much of the rails in the Shenandoah County, having already burned the railroad bridges at Tumbling Run, Pugh's Run, Narrow Passage and Edinburg. As late as 1863, railroad cars and railroad materials were still being hauled from Mount Jackson to Staunton and eventually to Richmond. Confederate records show that as many 180 wagonloads of "valuable rail scrap" were hauled from Mount Jackson to Staunton in the fall of 1863. In October 1864, the Federals reported finding burned-out engines and railcars at Woodstock.

3

The Unmentioned People

Blacks in the County

J ohn Wayland, a leading authority on the history of Shenandoah County, dismissed slavery as of little importance in the social and economic life of the county. According to Wayland:

> *Now and then a runaway slave might be caught and returned to his master, or another purchase his freedom or that of his wife; but slavery never fastened itself very deeply in Shenandoah County. Only a few of the proprietors had slaves; and, as a rule, only two or three on any one farm. This will explain why the county and the Valley as a whole recovered their economic strength so quickly following the Civil War.*

As evidence for his belief, Wayland relied on the low percentage of the slave population in Shenandoah County compared to the surrounding counties, as well as its dramatically lower percentage compared to the state as a whole. Wayland also saw the German heritage in Shenandoah County as a deterrent to slavery.

Recent scholarship, primarily from Nancy B. Stewart of Shenandoah County, has shown a much greater role for slavery in the cultural and economic life of antebellum Shenandoah County. Careful analysis of the 1860 census for Shenandoah County shows a direct correlation between wealth, slave ownership and political position. In Shenandoah County, as well as the surrounding counties, the majority of county leaders such as judges, magistrates, elected county officials and even the county sheriff were slave owners. Both of the Shenandoah County representatives to the Secession Convention in Richmond owned slaves, as did the generals in command of Shenandoah County regiments of the Virginia Militia. With few exceptions, the owners of hotels, manufacturing companies, stage lines and iron furnaces were all owners of slaves. While most gristmill owners did not own slaves, many of them rented slaves from time to time. Almost all of the largest landowners, especially those who owned the rich bottomland with its fertile soil, were slave owners.

Perhaps the finest estate with some of the best farmland in the county was Mount Airy, located south of Mount Jackson. In 1860, Mount Airy was owned by John G. Meem. Meem owned the largest number of slaves (thirty-six) in the county. Of Meem's thirty-six slaves, nine were children. The second-largest slave owner in the county was George Hupp of Strasburg. Hupp owned thirty slaves, including nine children. George Grandstaff, the owner of the Edinburg Mill, had twelve slaves, and the Allen family of Hawkinstown owned a total of twenty-three slaves divided among four families. The owners of the fine farm at Red Banks, William and Valentine Ripley, owned fifteen slaves between them. There were a number of other prominent families who held ten or more slaves, but the majority of owners held three or fewer slaves who worked alongside their owners planting and harvesting. Often, a family might own a slave couple, and the male would work in the fields with his owner while the female would help the farmer's wife with the daily housework. Some slaves also worked as house servants, and a number of older women owned at least one slave, probably to help out with daily activities.

SLAVE SALES

The black population in Shenandoah County reached its zenith in 1830, when there were 2,423 slaves in the county. From that point, the population of slaves decreased over the next thirty years. In 1860, the census reveals that there were 1,069 blacks in Shenandoah County, 753 of whom were slaves. This substantial decrease in the number of slaves over that thirty-year period is attributable to several factors. Some slaves simply died, but many more were born during that same period. A few slaves were freed by their masters, but the vast majority were simply sold and exported to the Deep South.

In Shenandoah County, slaves were often bought and sold between individuals, but from time to time, slave auctions were held at the county courthouse or one of the county's hotels or taverns. Many of these auctions were for the purpose of selling slaves to settle unpaid debt or delinquent taxes or as the result of the contents of a will. The local newspapers contain numerous advertisements for such auctions. Mark Bird of Woodstock was usually appointed by the court to supervise these sales. Following are the contents of such an advertisement:

> *Sale of Negroes belonging to Philip Pitman, sold 29th day of March 1858, by Mark Bird, trusted in a deed from said Pitman bearing the date 10th day of February 1854 and recorded in the Clerk's office of the Shenandoah County Court in Deed Book No 2, pages 55 and 56, to secure certain debts to the Bank in Staunton and to indemnify said Pitman's endorsers.*

Some deals were made with slave traders who advertised in newspapers or left advertisements in general stores. J.E. Carson from Augusta County regularly bought up Shenandoah County slaves for export. One of Carson's typical newspaper advertisements declared that he would pay high cash prices for "500 likely YOUNG NEGROES of both sexes, for the Southern market." In addition, Carson tracked down runaways and then purchased them cheap from their owners. Slave auctions sometimes caused families to be split apart, but county records show numerous instances when local buyers would purchase numerous family members in a sale to preserve family ties.

PREWAR EMANCIPATION

Early in Virginia history, the state legislature saw a problem with owners freeing slaves and allowing them to remain in the state. As far back as 1691, a law was passed that required emancipated persons to leave the state within six months of emancipation and required that their transportation to be paid by their slaveholders, otherwise the freed persons would face reenslavement. In practice, few slaveholders paid the transportation costs, and the free slaves remained illegally in the state. Newly freed slaves could appeal to the courts for permission to remain in the county, but few were successful. Freed slaves who did not have a visible means of support could be sold by the overseer of the poor for the benefit of the poor. County court records contain more than ninety cases where free blacks, usually children, were indentured to leading citizens to learn various trades. According to Shenandoah County court records, the last slave freed in the county before the Civil War was a male named James Allen, who was freed by the estate of Elizabeth Hickle.

WORKING RELATIONSHIPS BETWEEN SLAVES AND OTHERS

When discussing slavery in Shenandoah County, it is important to look at the fact that, of the 753 slaves in the county, only 466 of them were of prime working age. A prime working age slave in 1860 was considered to be one between twelve and sixty-five years of age. Working age slaves were almost evenly divided between male and female.

It is also important to note that slavery in Shenandoah County, while still reprehensible, could not in any way be compared to the cruel and despicable situation that often existed in the Deep South. The working relations between masters and slaves in Shenandoah County suggest a more complex and varied set of arrangements that sometimes suited the slave as well as the slave owner.

Farming was hard work and time-consuming, so many farmers either owned or rented slaves. Alert farmers, especially the bigger ones, were constantly searching for better ways to run their operations. Beginning in the 1820s, the *Woodstock Herald* advertised labor-saving devices such as the threshing machine, the corn sheller and the self-sharpening plough. Although these implements gradually changed farming methods in the valley, the major invention of the time was the reaper. Cyrus McCormick's reaper became available in 1831, and his improved model appeared in 1857. The reaper replaced the reaping hook or sickle, the cradle and the scythe, changing the methods of harvesting grain in the valley. Reaper salesmen claimed that "two men on the first reaper could cut as much grain in one day as 4–5 men with cradles or 12–16 men with reaping hooks." As more farmers acquired the reaper and learned better farming practices through the numerous agricultural societies that existed at that time, less slave labor was needed.

Tanneries, distilleries, merchant mills, gun makers, the textile industry and the iron industry used slaves, as well as free blacks. Slave labor was also used to maintain the Valley Pike, as well as other roads in the county. On these occasions, slaves worked right alongside white laborers. Industrial growth in the 1840s and 1850s depended heavily on slave labor, made more available by the expansion of slave hiring.

SLAVE HIRING

By the late antebellum period, slave hiring rivaled traditional slave ownership as the primary system of slavery in Virginia. In this practice, owners of a slave could "hire out" the slave to another employer. This allowed some farmers who did not have the means to purchase slaves to rent them for harvest and thus still profit from slave labor. On the other side, it allowed owners with idle slaves to make a profit from them.

Slave hiring in Shenandoah County took several forms. Many local slaves were hired out to others for specific tasks, such as wheat harvesting or planting. Some farm slaves, when idle on farms, were hired out to the iron furnaces, where work was less seasonal. In fact, iron furnaces were probably the main industry to employ slave hiring. For example, the 1860 census shows that Samuel Myers, co-owner of both Columbia Furnace and Henrietta Furnace, rented more than twenty slaves from other local owners for use at Columbia Furnace. That same census reveals that Myers owned only a single slave himself.

Slaveholders were able to rent out their slaves annually with payment averaging from 12 to 15 percent of the slaves' value, while the cost to hirers, or employers, was usually less than it would have cost for free workers. The going rate for a "day-laborer with board" in 1860 was $0.50. At this rate, free labor cost employers around $12.00 per month or nearly $140.00 per year. Slaves could be rented and boarded for as low as $80 a year—a substantial savings.

Early on, the practice of renting out slaves was relegated to unskilled laborers for jobs that involved intense labor. By the mid-nineteenth century, however, many skilled and semiskilled slaves were being hired out to blacksmith shops, tanneries and more specialized work in furnaces.

In some cases, employers could not find a sufficient number of slaves to hire in the local area, so they turned to the annual hiring markets held in Richmond and the Tidewater area. The two-week period following Christmas was the usual time for "slave hiring days," as the practice came to be known. Many skilled slaves had some say in whom they would work for and the types of work they would perform. They also got a percentage of what their masters received for their work. This was especially true in the iron industry. Tidewater slaves were eager to work in the valley because of the opportunity for overwork. Overwork provided the chance for slaves to earn money that they did not have to share with their owners.

Often, local slaves were allowed to hire themselves out to the highest bidder, and owners generally allowed slaves to keep a portion of the earnings from such labor. A few county slaveholders allowed their slaves to live on rented property and sell the crops they grew and keep all or part of the money. Others were allowed to acquire their own jobs and give the slaveholder one payment, keeping the rest for themselves. Some local slaveholders allowed slaves to "moonlight" for themselves. Documentation of such a situation is found in a claim with the Southern Claims Commission, filed by James H. Foster, a slave owned by Isaac S. Bowman. Foster testified:

> *I raised the hogs and purchased the cow, the carriage and harness from Charles J. Hite, a farmer who lived near Strasburg and who owned about 20 slaves. I was a shoemaker and used to work at my trade of nights for my own benefit; my master gave me the privilege. I had made shoes and repaired work for Mr. Hite and his slaves several years and took the cow, the carriage and harness from him in part payment of what he owed me and he was still owing me $125. I could not get.*

In 1860, merchant mills abounded in Shenandoah County, and mill owners regularly advertised to hire slave artisans and unskilled labor, even teenage boys who could handle light lifting and deliveries. Shenandoah County tavern owners and ordinaries usually had two or more "hands" to help with lodging, food and drink. At least one slave is thought to be buried in the small cemetery behind the Inn at Narrow Passage beside the grave of P. Stover, who died in 1850.

Some slaves and free blacks lived in the same house with white families. Others lived in the small building near the family home, sometimes called the "summer kitchen." A close relationship developed in homes where black women, free or slave, served as housekeepers or "nurses" for children.

THREATS OF SLAVERY

The enslavement of blacks always presented certain threats to the white population. Slaves sometimes revolted, killing their masters and creating havoc in the area. In 1831, Nat Turner, a slave in Southampton County, Virginia, led a slave rebellion that resulted in the deaths of sixty whites, including many women and children. Turner was eventually captured, sentenced to death and hanged. In the aftermath, the state executed fifty-six blacks accused of being part of Turner's slave rebellion. Two hundred blacks were also beaten and killed by white militias and mobs reacting to the violence. In Virginia and other Southern states, legislators passed new laws prohibiting the education of slaves, restricting rights of assembly and even requiring white ministers to be present at black worship services. Slaves who traveled from one place to another were required to carry passes signed by their owners. Those without such a pass could be arrested and jailed as a runaway.

The Virginia militia law of 1858 was created in part because of the fear of slave revolts. It was also at this time that many counties established or enhanced their slave patrols. In Shenandoah County, the slave patrols were appointed by the court, which meant their activities, as a pseudo police force, were legally sanctioned. Slave owners relied on the slave patrols to act as a form of law enforcement to monitor the activities of slaves and keep a watchful eye on any potential rebellions. The court appointed specific persons for the slave patrol on a regular basis.

The fear of a slave revolt increased exponentially on October 16, 1859, when the abolitionist John Brown raided the Federal arsenal at Harpers Ferry in hopes of beginning a massive slave insurrection throughout the Southern states. Although Brown and his followers were quickly cornered and captured, the ramifications of the attack on the secession debate were enormous. Brown's attack seemed to confirm suspicions about Northern fanaticism on the slavery issue. The *Republican Vindicator*, a Staunton newspaper, claimed that documents found on Brown's person "demonstrated beyond all shadow of a doubt the existence of a widespread conspiracy of the North for the forcible suppression of Southern slavery." In the Deep South, cries for secession grew louder.

Nervous excitement in the county grew as the rift between North and South grew larger. Newspapers whipped up the population on both sides of the slavery issue. The election of 1860 promised a bitter political debate that would likely harden positions on both sides and force Shenandoah County to come to terms with the secession crisis. In the county and Virginia as a whole, the population began to separate into three distinct groups: the secessionists, who advocated immediate withdrawal from the United States; the unionists, who believed that the crisis could be solved within the Union; and the conditional unionists, who advocated remaining in the Union so long as the Federal government could protect Virginia's rights.

4

Road to Division

In part because of its heavy settlement from Pennsylvania, the Shenandoah Valley has been called "a world between" or the "third South," where according to some historians there was little commitment to the Southern cause in the Civil War and even less to the institution of slavery.

The idea of the Shenandoah Valley as exceptional to the South is understandable but was certainly not the case in much of antebellum Shenandoah County. Shenandoah County had fewer slaves than the other Shenandoah Valley counties, yet its residents seem to have had a stronger early commitment to secession and slavery than their valley neighbors. County voters supported Breckinridge, the Southern candidate, in the election of 1860 when most valley counties supported Bell, the unionist candidate. They selected two pro-secession candidates to the state Secession Convention in Richmond when its neighboring counties selected more moderate candidates. And as mentioned earlier, most of the leading citizens in the county were slave owners who had an economic and social interest in the preservation of slavery.

RELUCTANT SECESSIONISTS

Shenandoah County was home to a substantial number of people who opposed slavery and separation from the Union. Their numbers were small, and their hazards many, yet they managed to maintain their own loyalties and take opportunities to oppose slavery and secession whenever they could. When war came, these same people helped slaves trying to escape and aided those trying to avoid the Confederate draft. They provided information to the Federal army whenever possible and took care of wounded Federals when they could. Theirs was perhaps the most hazardous trial of all, for they came to fear both their neighbors and sometimes undiscerning Yankees who thought all valley people were the same.

Perhaps the most well known of those who opposed slavery in the county was George Rye. George Rye was a prosperous Shenandoah County saddler and politician who was a strong advocate of abolitionism. As early as 1837, George Rye was charged with "feloniously writing, printing, and causing to be written and printed a persuasive writing with the intent of advising, enticing and persuading persons of color within the Commonwealth of Virginia to make insurrection and to rebel and denying the right of masters to property in their slaves and inculcating the duty of resistance to such right contrary to the form of statue in such case made and provided." That case continued in the courts until July 1840, when the court dismissed the charges.

In June 1856, George Rye attended the first National Republican Convention in Philadelphia, where, according to the *Philadelphia Inquirer* newspaper, during a speech Rye made disparaging remarks about Virginia and its position on slavery. Local newspapers angrily condemned Rye's remarks as insulting and libelous. Vociferous parts of the Woodstock population were outraged, and on July 4, 1856, Rye was burned in effigy. Three days later, Rye was the subject of an "indignation" meeting where Samuel C. Williams, secretary of the meeting, called Rye "a viper in their bosoms." The meeting resolved that Rye should be "cast out…by the lynch law, if necessary." In 1860, Rye was again threatened with expulsion from the county because of his support for Abraham Lincoln.

At the beginning of the Civil War, George Rye, age fifty-one, was too old for the military draft. He remained in the county throughout the war and, soon after the end of war, was elected presiding justice in the Shenandoah County Court. Rye subsequently served in a variety of posts in the Reconstruction government. In 1876, Judge Rye donated the arched entrance gate with angels at Cedarwood Cemetery.

THE ELECTION OF 1860

The year 1860 held perhaps the most important presidential election in the history of the United States. The issue of secession, talked about for years, was at the forefront of the minds of much of the population. The battles in Congress were epic as congressmen fought over a variety of sectional issues, including the proposed Morrill Tariff with its protective import taxes favoring Northern industry over Southern agriculture. Southerners worried about the shifting balance of power as the Northern states achieved more seats in the House of Representatives. Matters were made worse by the growing power abolitionists were gaining over public opinion in the North. In the South, slave owners were increasingly fearful of slave uprisings after the Nat Turner insurrection and John Brown's attack at Harpers Ferry.

The spirit of compromise that had existed in the past was gone. The Democratic Party was not even able to select a single candidate to represent the party. Southern Democrats split off from the main party and selected John C. Breckinridge as their candidate, while the rest of the party backed Senator Stephen Douglas from Illinois. The Constitutional Union Party, only recently established, selected John Bell of Tennessee. The Republican Party selected Abraham Lincoln, also from Illinois. The abolitionists were an important part of the Republican Party, and Lincoln had frequently spoken about the evils of slavery. Many Southern politicians and newspaper editors believed the election of Lincoln would mean the end of slavery.

As the election year approached, sectionalism increased all over Virginia. In the Northwest, ardent unionists pledged to support the Northern Democrat, Stephen Douglas, while easterners favored the Southern Democrat, John Breckinridge, or the Constitutional Union Party and John Bell. Abraham Lincoln, the Republican candidate, lacked substantial support in any part of Virginia.

Election day came, and the votes were cast. Breckinridge won the majority of votes in Shenandoah County, receiving 1,883, or almost 75.53 percent of the total votes. Bell carried the state but received only 427 votes in Shenandoah County. Douglas received only 170 votes, while only 13 brave souls voted for Lincoln. Frederick and Page Counties joined Shenandoah in supporting Breckinridge, but Rockingham and Augusta Counties voted heavily for Bell.

Lincoln won the election, setting up a national crisis that could split the country. Lincoln's election led South Carolina and the other states of the Deep South to set the wheels of secession in motion. Thoughtful leaders on both sides worked to bridge the gap between the North and South. Shenandoah County joined in the attempt to keep the Union together. The November 16, 1860 edition of the *Richmond Daily Examiner* reported that, "on November 12, a public meeting in Shenandoah County demanded the calling of a convention to confer with other slave states in an effort to gain concessions from the North sufficient to keep the lower South in the Union." Nothing came of this meeting, and the county, like the rest of the Union, spent the remainder of 1860 watching and waiting for the next move.

On December 20, 1860, South Carolina delegates voted to repeal the state's ratification of the U.S. Constitution, effectively seceding from the Union. Within a few weeks, most of the other states in the Deep South also seceded and formed the Confederacy, with its capital in Montgomery, Alabama. Virginia and the other slave states still in the Union were in a difficult political position. Governor Letcher wanted to remain in the Union, but events beyond his control were taking place. On January 15, 1861, in response to a vote by the state legislature, Letcher called a convention to consider the issue of Virginia secession. The Virginia General Assembly, in ordering the convention, asked voters to decide whether the convention, if it chose to secede, had to submit its decision to the voters in a popular referendum.

Shenandoah County voters elected Colonel Raphael Morgan Conn and Samuel Crousden Williams as its delegates to the Secession Convention. Conn was then the sheriff of Shenandoah County and the colonel of the Forty-third Regiment of Virginia Militia, although the organization was never mustered.

Samuel Crousden Williams, of Woodstock, had been clerk of the Circuit Court of Shenandoah County since 1845. He was an experienced politician, having served in the Virginia General Assembly and as a member of the Virginia Constitutional Convention of 1850. Both Williams and Conn were slaveholders.

For the next two months, county citizens anxiously watched for news from the convention. Thirty of the convention delegates were known to be secessionists, thirty were avowed unionists and ninety-two were moderates who were not clearly identified with either of the first two groups. After Lincoln's inaugural address on March 4 and the failure of the Washington Peace Conference, it became clear that Abraham Lincoln intended to use force to maintain the Union. Even in the face of the evidence of Lincoln's intentions, the convention held its first vote on April 4, and the majority of delegates voted to remain in the Union. Despite the fact that most valley counties voted to remain in the Union, both Shenandoah County delegates voted for secession, as did the delegates from Page and Warren County. On April 7, the convention received word that Lincoln had decided to resupply Fort Sumter, and six days later, the first shots of the American Civil War exploded over Charleston Harbor. On April 15, Lincoln issued a call for seventy-five thousand volunteers to suppress the rebellion. This call for troops was the last straw for the conditional unionists, and on April 17, the convention voted eighty-eight to fifty-five in favor of secession. Even at this point, twelve of the valley's nineteen delegates still voted against secession. All that remained was to await the results of the referendum.

The referendum took place on Thursday, May 23, but by then open opposition to secession had virtually disappeared in most of Virginia. In Shenandoah County, 2,513 people voted for the ordinance of secession, while only 5 voted against it. Residents who voted against Virginia's secession were William Moreland from Fort Valley, Walter Craig from Mount Jackson, Walter Newman of Liberty Furnace and Jacob W. and Sarah A. Wine, husband and wife, from Forestville. Since emotions were running high and acts of violence and vandalism were already occurring against Unionists and antislavery activists, it must have taken a great deal of courage to even consider voting against secession when all votes were a matter of public record.

The fact that only five citizens voted against the ordinance of secession should not be taken as evidence that the county was in complete support of secession. Written evidence exists in diaries, family histories and especially sworn statements in the Southern Claims Commission files that more citizens would have voted against the ordinance, but hostile and sometimes unruly mobs intimidated them with threats of injury or even death. Others claimed to have voted for the ordinance under duress. Other citizens simply stayed away from the polls. At that time, voters cast an oral vote before county officials in a public forum. There were no secret ballots, so how a citizen voted was soon known throughout the community.

The troubles for those who supported the Union in Shenandoah County were only beginning. Over the next few years, they would suffer the wrath of many of their neighbors, loss of their property and, in some cases, even death.

5

The County Goes to War

When war came, many young men in the county quickly stepped forward to stand with Virginia. They rapidly filled the volunteer companies being organized in the county, several of which would become part of the fabled Stonewall Brigade. A few of these companies marched off to Harpers Ferry without uniforms, weapons or accoutrements. At Harpers Ferry, they were armed and organized into regiments. When Virginia joined the Confederacy, the county soldiers were transferred into the Confederate army. Richmond became the new Confederate capital. Each county was given a quota of volunteers needed for the Confederate military forces, which Shenandoah County quickly met.

Shenandoah County women quickly stepped up to support their men and their state. When Virginia joined the Confederacy, the majority of these ladies became ardent supporters of the new nation. At the Union Church in Mount Jackson, as well as dozens of other places, women gathered to make uniforms for their men. Linen was gathered and sewn into tents; socks and undergarments were made by hand in large numbers. As fabric that had generally been made in the North or imported from Europe disappeared from the shelves of stores, women revived the skill of weaving or turned to wool to produce clothing and blankets needed by men on the front.

With many of the younger men away with the army, older men, children and women took over more of the duties in the field and pasture. Fortunately for local families, much of the spring planting had already been completed, but planting represented only a portion of the arduous work that had to

Union Church in Mount Jackson. The church was used for many purposes during the war.

be done on a daily basis. In many cases, other members of the community pitched in to help one another. On the homefront, those who kept the farms producing were crucial to the war effort. The importance of Shenandoah County iron production rose dramatically when the war began. Tredegar Ironworks in Richmond was the most importance munitions producer in the Confederacy early in the war, and it needed copious amounts of pig iron to produce iron plates for the CSS *Virginia*, as well as for cannons and artillery shells. Contracts were quickly made with Shenandoah County iron producers to furnish large amounts of this vital material. Early in the war, highly skilled ironworkers were exempted from the draft in order to keep the furnaces and forges operating. Unfortunately, many of the county furnaces did not achieve their potential, so Tredegar actually assumed control of several of these operations. Two Fort Valley furnaces were taken over by Tredegar. Horses were the backbone of Civil War transportation, so wagon builders, saddlers and harness makers were also vital to the war effort. Shoemakers and tanners were also critical, so a number of skilled county artisans were detailed back to their homes to do these kinds of work.

ACTIONS IN 1861

On April 17, 1861, units of the Virginia Militia seized the Federal armory and arsenal at Harpers Ferry. Harpers Ferry quickly became the center for organizing and training many of the South's future soldiers. Newly recruited companies, including those from Shenandoah County, marched off to Harpers Ferry to begin the process of becoming soldiers.

When Virginia formally joined the Confederacy, Major General Joseph E. Johnston was appointed as commander of the forces in the Shenandoah Valley, and Thomas J. Jackson, now a brigadier general, was given command of the newly created First Brigade, which then included the Second, Fourth, Fifth and Twenty-seventh Virginia Infantry Regiments. A short time later, the Thirty-third Infantry was added. The county also contributed a company to the Tenth Virginia Infantry. Several companies of cavalry were also recruited during this period and assigned to what became known as Ashby's cavalry. The Eight Star Artillery was formed in New Market and was quickly marched off to the western part of the state.

The militiamen from Shenandoah County were members of one of three regiments: the 13th, the 136th or the 146th. These units formed part of the 7th Brigade of Virginia Militia commanded by Brigadier General Gilbert S. Meem of Mount Jackson. All three Shenandoah County militia regiments were called up and marched to the fairgrounds at Winchester, where they went into camp. For the next two months, militiamen were shuffled back and forth between Martinsburg and Winchester, sometimes on military maneuvers and sometimes as labor assisting in the removal of the captured railroad equipment. Meem, along with the other militia generals, was relieved, and more experienced officers took command.

In July 1861, most Shenandoah soldiers experienced their first real combat, and they made an excellent accounting for themselves. County boys were part of Jackson's force that rode the rails to Manassas Junction. As soon as they arrived, they were marched straight into the reserve, and within three hours, they would be in the thick of the fight. The Confederates only achieved victory thanks to those reinforcements from the Shenandoah Valley. It was during this battle that Jackson earned the nickname "Stonewall" when Brigadier General Barnard Bee of South Carolina pointed to Jackson's troops and shouted, "There stands Jackson like a stone wall!" The charge of the Thirty-third Virginia Infantry, including the Emerald Guard, probably did as much to win the battle as any regiment on the field that day, but for that valor it paid a terrible price. The Battle of First Manassas convinced both sides that this was not going to be a short war. The news of the heroic part played by the local companies was offset to a great degree by a long list of the killed and wounded. Citizens gathered around the telegraph office, an event that would be relived every time a battle took place, to read the casualty lists as they came across the lines. About 10 percent of the 387 Confederate dead at First Manassas came from Shenandoah County.

In the fall of 1861, Richmond transferred General Jackson back to the valley, giving him command of the Valley District. Jackson, along with a small staff, traveled to Winchester, where he established his headquarters. Jackson then began the job of creating a suitable fighting force to defend the valley. Aside from Ashby's cavalry, most of Jackson's command consisted of militia. To augment his force, Jackson requested and received his former brigade, which would go down in history as the "Stonewall Brigade." Richmond also reassigned the three other poorly led brigades, but they proved to be of little use. Jackson attempted to regain some control of the northwestern counties, conducting an ill-fated campaign into that area. Although he successfully captured Romney, the freezing weather and recalcitrant officers combined to stymie Jackson's efforts to hold the area.

6

Caring for the Sick
and Wounded

During the war, thousands of sick and wounded soldiers were treated
and cared for in Shenandoah County. In addition to the soldiers who
became sick or were wounded in the county, thousands of Southern troops
from the battlefields of Manassas, Antietam, Winchester and Gettysburg
were brought to Shenandoah County for treatment. But it was not only
soldiers in gray who were treated here; many soldiers in blue also received
care in the churches and homes of the county.

Because of its strategic location, Strasburg was occupied by the Federals
for several months early in the war. While there, the Federals established a
large hospital in and around the Presbyterian church to house their soldiers
suffering from a variety of diseases. In May 1862, 1,015 Federal troops were
reported as sick in Strasburg.

Strasburg's proximity to the battlefield of Cedar Creek in October 1864
caused the little town to be inundated with wounded and dying soldiers from
both sides. As happened so often, area homes became makeshift hospitals.
The Daniel Stickley home, located north of the town on the Valley Pike, was
quickly commandeered to treat the wounded. Soon, casualties poured into
the Stickley farm. According to information from the Shenandoah County
Sesquicentennial Committee:

> Surgeons [were] *performing so many amputations that the pile of limbs*
> *reached higher than the family dining table on which the operations took*
> *place. Today, that same pine table can be found in the National Museum*
> *of Civil War Medicine located in Frederick, Maryland.*

The Stickley home near Cedar Creek. This home was used as a hospital following the Battle of Cedar Creek.

The Barbe home, located at the foot of Fisher's Hill, sheltered the wounded following the Battle of Fisher's Hill on September 22, 1864. Following the end of fighting, hundreds of wounded soldiers were brought to the farm. The home, the yard and all the outbuildings were filled to overflowing with bleeding and battered men wearing both the blue and the gray uniforms. At least thirty wounded men were lain side by side on the long, wide porch to the side of the house. The Barbe House, a beautifully appointed brick home, still stands today, as do several of the stone outbuildings.

THE CONFEDERATE HOSPITAL IN MOUNT JACKSON

The largest medical facility in Shenandoah County was the Confederate hospital in Mount Jackson. In 1861, the Confederate Medical Department authorized the construction of a Confederate hospital in Mount Jackson. The location seems to have been selected because it was serviced by the railroad but far enough away from the contending armies to be a safe haven for sick and wounded soldiers. A local businessman, Colonel Levi Rinker, donated land for the hospital, as well as for two cemeteries soon laid out near the hospital. The hospital complex, probably built by master bridge builder John Woods, was located north of Mount Jackson. Sitting parallel to the Valley Pike and very near the railroad, the hospital was convenient for the transfer of the sick or wounded. A Massachusetts soldier described the hospital complex as it looked in late April 1962:

> The buildings were admirably contrived and constructed. In addition to two or three small ones, there were two completed and one nearly so, of perhaps a hundred and fifty feet in length, two stories in height, perfectly ventilated, and yet warm…the hospital flags still flying, but the 500 sick Rebels convalescing there had been removed ten days previous.

In addition to the hospital buildings were several staff houses, a kitchen building and a number of outbuildings. One of the buildings had a large cupola adorning its roof.

Previous page, bottom: The Barbe House, located on the Fisher's Hill Battlefield. Hundreds of wounded men from both sides were treated here following the battle on September 22, 1864.

Harrison House, home of Dr. Andrew Meem in Mount Jackson during the war.

The medical director at the Mount Jackson Hospital was Dr. A.R. Meem. Dr. Meem was a graduate of Princeton University and the University of Pennsylvania Medical College. He was a member of the prominent Meem family, owners of the Mount Airy estate located in Meem's Bottoms.

Dr. Meem and his wife, Anne Jordon Meem, lived during much of the war in a fine brick home in Mount Jackson loaned to them by Colonel Ricker, chief benefactor of the hospital. That home is now known as the Harrison House. Early in 1864, Meem served in the general hospital at Harrisonburg but apparently returned to Mount Jackson. Dr. Meem became ill of an unknown ailment on a visit to Harrisonburg, Virginia, on February 26, 1865, and died there at the age of forty-one.

Early in the war, the hospital was mainly used to treat illnesses, particularly typhoid fever, which seemed to be the most prevalent at that time. Following the First Battle of Manassas, large numbers of wounded soldiers were brought in by the MGRR, which was still operational at that time. Sick and wounded from the early valley campaigns and the 1862 invasion of Maryland were also brought to Mount Jackson. The hospital in Mount Jackson was classified as a wayside hospital, which meant it was never intended as a permanent treatment facility for the badly wounded. Instead, it was used to care for those who could not make the fifty-mile trip to the

General and Receiving Hospital in Staunton. The hospital treated at least one hundred patients almost every month for the first two years of war. Dr. Meem reported his concern over the high mortality rate at his hospital to the Medical Department in Richmond, but there was little that could be done because of the critical shortages of medicine and supplies throughout the South.

The hospital was ignored by the department after the fall of 1862 even though the facility was continuing to care for Confederate soldiers. Only four nurses, all convalescing soldiers, were present to assist Meem as late as June 30, 1863. The first soldiers taken to Mount Jackson following the Battle of Gettysburg had to be directed on immediately to Staunton because of the hospital's lack of supplies and personnel.

Unaware that Dr. Meem was still at the Mount Jackson hospital, a new medical director, Dr. Robert F. Baldwin of Winchester, was appointed. Mount Jackson was to be used to treat those too sick or too badly wounded to survive the trip to Staunton. Dr. Meem, whose whereabouts were still unknown by the Medical Department, was ordered to "report to Mt. Jackson" to serve as one of Baldwin's surgeons. Meem, of course, had never left Mount Jackson. Eleven convalescent soldiers from Staunton were assigned as medical attendants and ward masters. Nine more were assigned as nurses.

Because of the summer heat, twenty-five tents were sent to the hospital to shelter the patients. In the wake of the retreat from Gettysburg, Mount Jackson was taxed to the limit. Approximately 8,500 wounded Confederate soldiers, plus 4,000 Union prisoners, passed along the Valley Pike. In July, 667 patients, including 215 suffering from gunshot wounds, were hospitalized in Mount Jackson. The rest were victims of typhoid, diarrhea, dysentery, pneumonia, debilitus and rheumatism. Remarkably, only thirteen patients died in July.

Periodically, the Union army took over the hospital, including during the aftermath of the Battle of New Market (May 15, 1864). Surgeon Alexander Neil of the Twelfth West Virginia Infantry noted in a letter to his family that "we brought away two or three hundred of our wounded, filled three hospital buildings in Mt. Jackson and with our whole medical force worked hard with them until sometime in the night, many mortally wounded dying on our hands." General Hunter reported that many Federal soldiers were still being cared for at the hospital when he occupied Mount Jackson in early June 1864.

Following Early's defeat at Fisher's Hill, he withdrew to Mount Jackson, where he placed the remnants of his four infantry divisions in a line of battle astride the pike near the hospital. While the infantry waited for the Federals to attack, Early ordered the medical supplies removed from the hospital. When Sheridan's cavalry appeared in his front, Early withdrew his army. As the Federals entered Mount Jackson, they noted that the hospitals were filled with Confederate wounded. The single building of the hospital complex that was not occupied was set on fire and destroyed. In the summer of 1865, an occupation force, the 192nd Ohio Volunteer Infantry, tore down the hospital buildings and used the lumber to build a temporary military installation at Rude's Hill.

Directly across the pike from the site of the hospital lies a Confederate cemetery known as Our Soldiers Cemetery. Our Soldiers Cemetery was established in 1861 to bury Confederate soldiers who died in the hospitals around Mount Jackson. Colonel Levi Rinker donated the land for the cemetery. The earliest burials in the Confederate cemetery date from September 1861.

The cemetery, containing over 450 graves, was first dedicated on May 10, 1866, by a memorial association organized by a group of local ladies. The entire community, including the nearby towns of New Market and Edinburg, participated in the dedication of the cemetery. A wreath of flowers was placed on each of the graves. The ceremonies included addresses in the church by Major H.K. Douglas (an aide of General Stonewall Jackson) and others.

In 1897, the Mount Jackson Chapter of the United Daughters of the Confederacy was organized to care for the cemetery and erect a monument. Within six years, it was able to raise $1,500 to erect a white marble statue of a Confederate soldier that sits in the middle of the cemetery. This statue was erected and dedicated in 1903.

Located just across the railroad track from Our Soldiers Cemetery is a small cemetery where the African Americans who died in the area were buried. It is generally believed that this cemetery was laid out about the same time as the Confederate cemetery, also on land donated by Colonel Levi Rinker.

After the Battle of New Market on May 15, 1864, practically the whole town of New Market became a hospital. Nearly every suitable structure became a hospital, including many home and barns. The Smith Creek Baptist Church near New Market was turned into a hospital for wounded Federals. Dr. Rice's home and barn sheltered the wounded from both sides. Even Mount Airy, near to Mount Jackson, was used for the care of the casualties. The Cedar Grove church on Rude's Hill was used as a hospital for hundreds of Federal troops.

Caring for the Sick and Wounded

Entrance to Our Soldiers Cemetery located in Mount Jackson.

Cedar Grove Church, used by Federal doctors to treat the wounded from the Battle of New Market.

Confederate surgeons, together with the local doctors, spent a long night caring for the wounded. Local citizens gave graciously in this time of need. The ladies tore their bed linens into strips to be used for bandages and assisted as nurses on the field and in their homes. Jessie Hainning Rupert, a native of Pittsfield, Massachusetts, who did not hide her Union sympathies from her New Market neighbors, together with her husband, Solomon, brought in Federal wounded to their house. When the house was filled, they moved additional wounded into an empty warehouse nearby. After the battle, she wrote, "The night passed wearily away. There was no peace in its dark hours. All the glory of victory seemed quickly melted away in the grim aftermath of pain and death."

Mrs. Eliza Clinedinst Crim worked to tend to wounded cadets. Years later, Mrs. Eliza Clinedinst Crim recalled:

> *I stayed up all night to help with the wounded. We helped to carry the wounded into the old Rice home. We made a fire and gave them warm drinks, but many died that night...They told me a poor little cadet [was] lying down at the Lightfoot Farm, badly wounded...He laid there all night*

Maryland House at Orkney Springs. This building was an original part of the Orkney Springs hotel where Southern troops came to recuperate.

but in the morning after the battle [Cadet] *Moses Ezekiel brought him to my home...My old mother put him in her own bed, as it was the only bed we had downstairs...* [Three days later] *he died about midnight in Moses Ezekiel's arms.*

The cadet was Thomas Garland Jefferson, whose quick action saved the life of his fellow cadet on the day of the battle. The cadets still remember Eliza as the "Mother of VMI Cadets," a tribute to the manner in which she tended to their wounded comrades.

Certainly, the most peaceful place in the county to recuperate was near the mineral springs at the resort of Orkney Springs. The original hotel at Orkney Springs, now known as the Maryland House, was never an active hospital; however, a number of Confederate soldiers were allowed to recuperate there.

It was not only soldiers who were affected by diseases during the war. Smallpox and typhoid fever cases spread across the county as soldiers from both sides came through. Cases of disease were particularly prevalent in Mount Jackson, probably spread by soldiers being treated there for similar ailments. A similar situation existed in Strasburg, where several large Federal hospitals were in use in the spring of 1862. Residents in the Fort Valley were hard hit with diseases probably brought by the soldiers who returned home on leave.

7

Federals Invade the County

The year 1862 saw the most dramatic Confederate victories in the Shenandoah Valley and cemented the reputation of General Stonewall Jackson as a master strategist. Those victories could not have come at a better time because early that year the war was not going well for the South. Southern harbors were already being blockaded, and New Orleans, the largest port in the South, had fallen to Federal forces. In Tennessee, Forts Henry and Donelson were also in Federal hands.

In Washington, Major General George B. McClellan was poised for an attack into Virginia with more than 110,000 well-trained troops, while Major General Irvin McDowell readied another 40,000 men for action. Lincoln, under tremendous political pressure to end the war, prodded McClellan to capture Richmond and take Virginia out of the war. To capture Richmond, McClellan came up with a complex plan involving the coordinated efforts of several Federal armies at one time. McClellan intended to land on the Virginia coast, swiftly move west and attack Richmond from the east. McClellan expected that Johnston would be forced to move back to Richmond, and then McDowell's army would move directly south and attack Richmond from the north in conjunction with McClellan's attack from the east.

Lincoln approved the plan but insisted that the small Confederate force stationed in the Shenandoah Valley must first be neutralized. The Confederates in the valley had already ruined the chances for a Federal victory at First Manassas.

Watching the Federal buildup, Johnston abandoned his positions around Centerville and Manassas, moving first to the Rappahannock River and then to Richmond upon learning that McClellan's army had landed below Yorktown. Johnston left one division under Richard Ewell in the piedmont to protect the area.

To drive Jackson's little army out of the valley, Washington selected the forces under the command of Major General Nathaniel Banks. Banks left his camps in Frederick, Maryland, and slowly marched to the Potomac, where he crossed and entered the valley. (This would soon be his undoing.) Banks was a better politician than a soldier, but following his orders, he began to advance cautiously up the valley. He managed to take Winchester on March 11 without a real fight as Jackson, outnumbered five to one, reluctantly abandoned his "adopted hometown" and marched his little army to Strasburg. Jackson's headquarters were established at the large brick mansion owned by George F. Hupp. The Hupp mansion would subsequently be used by general officers of both sides many times throughout the rest of the war.

Home of Israel Allen, where Jackson spent time in 1862.

Richmond's orders to Jackson were simple: protect the heart of the valley and keep Banks's troops from being drawn off to support the campaign against Richmond. A Federal penetration deep into the valley would cut Confederate supply lines and disrupt recruiting efforts. Allowing the Federals to move troops east would increase the difficulty of defending Richmond.

Confederate infantry remained near Strasburg until March 15, when Banks marched out of Winchester and headed for Shenandoah County. Jackson then continued south to the Hawkinstown area, where he established his headquarters at the large home of Israel Allen, while much of his infantry went into camp at Camp Buchanan in Red Banks.

TURNER ASHBY: THE BLACK KNIGHT

Turner Ashby, born on October 23, 1828, in Fauquier County, was a soldier by nature. He came from a family with four generations of military service, although Ashby never received any formal military training. His first military service came in 1857, when he raised a company of volunteers to police the workers building the railroad through the gap in the Blue Ridge Mountains. When John Brown made his attack at Harpers Ferry, Ashby and his volunteer cavalry were among the first to respond. They remained on duty in Harpers Ferry until after the trial and execution of Brown and his men.

At the start of the war, Ashby was commissioned as a captain. Along with his old company, now an official part of the Virginia forces, Ashby returned Harpers Ferry, where he became familiar to Jackson. His command, known as the Ashby Rangers, became part of the Seventh Virginia Cavalry. By June 1861, he had been promoted to the rank of lieutenant colonel in command of ten companies. Young men from some of the best families of western Virginia rushed to join his command. He employed the first battery of horse artillery used in the war. In 1862, he was promoted to the rank of colonel. On May 23, 1862, he was promoted to the rank of brigadier general, probably at Jackson's office next to the courthouse in Woodstock, and given command of the Ashby Brigade. This brigade became famous throughout the war; in 1864, it was given the name "Laurel Brigade."

A man of striking personal appearance, General Ashby was about five feet, ten inches tall, well proportioned, graceful and compact, with black hair and eyes, a black beard and a dark complexion. He was a calm, gentle man, not given to drinking or swearing. He often smiled but rarely laughed,

Lawyers' Row in Woodstock. The office in the background was used by Stonewall Jackson in 1862.

especially after the death of his brother Richard, who died as a result of wounds he received in an encounter with a Union patrol early in the war.

Following the death of his brother, Turner became a changed man. His life was consecrated to the cause of the South, and he risked all in the service of his country. Ashby displayed an unusual coolness and determination in battle. The sight of Ashby galloping over the battlefield on his black stallion or Tom Telegraph, his favorite white horse, became a familiar one to friend and foe alike. Ashby seemed to never tire. It is said that Ashby would sometimes ride sixty to eighty miles in a single day. The activity and physical endurance of Ashby were fireside talks in his camps. The popularity of the cavalry service attracted young men, and his command increased to twenty-six companies. Ashby's restless and energetic spirit left little time to properly organize, train and instill discipline in the numerous new cavalry companies joining his command. Turner Ashby was never a strict disciplinarian. He relied on his personal courage and charisma to get his men to follow him. Unlike the infantry, Ashby's cavalry was in constant motion and in almost daily contact with the enemy. The immediate necessities of the military situation and the free-wheeling character of the men who made up his command made an efficient organization an almost impossible task. The companies were often widely separated so that a compact regimental organization was impossible; in fact, at no time during the campaign of 1862 were all these companies united for a combined attack.

Early in the war, Ashby's cavalry was also poorly equipped. Many of his men were armed with double-barreled shotguns or old flintlock pistols and muskets. Modern sabers were scarce. Stories abound that some of Ashby's men actually went into combat armed only with clubs.

What Ashby's cavalry lacked in discipline and equipment was made up for with excellent horsemanship, tremendous spirit and a strong faith in their leader. Their dash and fury in the cavalry charge brought fear into an enemy unprepared by either training or experience for attack by a cavalry force. Ashby's tactics and strategy were so unorthodox that he confused his opponents and held them in check by their ignorance of his strength and purpose.

One of Ashby's finest weapons was a battery of horse artillery, commanded by Captain R. Preston Chew, a young graduate of the Virginia Military Institute. Early in the war, Chew's battery contained only three guns, but one of them, an English-made Blakely, became famous in the valley. Several Confederate soldiers referred in letters and diaries to the "bark of the Blakely."

Ashby's cavalry and artillery were responsible for protecting the rear of Jackson's army and delaying Banks's advance. The numerous creeks and rolling hills over which the Valley Pike crossed were tailor made for delaying actions by a small force, and Ashby took full advantage of this. On March 18, 1862, Ashby determined to defend the approaches to the bridge at Cedar Creek. Chew's battery was placed on the high hill south of the bridge. As the Federal columns came into view, Ashby's troopers set fire to the covered bridge and began firing on the lead element. The Federals withdrew before reaching the creek. With the help of a local black man, they found a ford upstream where they crossed. Ashby then retired to Strasburg, having accomplished his purpose of delay. Ashby's men grabbed a few hours of much-needed rest and at dawn took up another defensive position at the top of Fisher's Hill. Private George M. Neese of New Market, a member of Chew's battery, recalled the events of March 19:

> *Early this morning we moved to the top of Fisher's Hill, two miles above Strasburg, put our battery in a good commanding position, and awaited the*

advance of the enemy. We did not have to wait long before their advance guard appeared over Hupp's Hill, nearly a mile north of Strasburg. Close behind their advance guard came their artillery and infantry, with steady tread, in solid column, and in overwhelming numbers. We had nothing but one battery and Ashby's regiment of cavalry to oppose the mighty host that was approaching with floating banners...They marched in one body until they arrived in town. Then one column flanked out on their right and advanced up the railroad and the other came up the pike. When the one on the pike came within range of our guns, we opened fire on the head of the column, which checked, mixed, and muddled them, and they retired, not quite in as good dress parade order as they had advanced just a moment before. But in the meantime the column that came up the railroad was about flanking our position, and about a mile northeast of us they put an eight-gun battery in position at almost the same altitude as ours.

When they opened fire on us with eight guns—and from the clear-cut whiz of the shell they were all rifled pieces at that—with an infantry column advancing on our left and one in the front—eight rifled guns playing on two—we quickly arrived at the conclusion that discretion being the better part of valor, we would retire without delay. We fell back about a mile and took another position. The enemy advanced their battery, and we opened on them again. They returned our fire, doubling the amount. We fell back to another position and opened again, and they also repeated their tactics, and so we kept on falling back, firing at them from every hilltop for six miles.

When we left our last position it was nearly night, and we came to Narrow Passage, three miles south of Woodstock, and camped for the night. The Yanks fell back to Strasburg, which is twelve miles from Woodstock.

From his camp at Narrow Passage, Ashby followed Banks back down the Valley Pike to Kernstown just south of Winchester. From local people, Ashby learned that Banks was breaking up his force, sending a large part of it east to Washington. Here, Ashby made one of his few mistakes in reconnaissance, for he seriously underestimated the strength of the Federal forces remaining at Kernstown. Ashby rushed back to Jackson and informed him of the Federal withdrawal. Jackson immediately set his force into motion, marching with little rest to reach the Federal position before additional forces could be sent east. On March 23, Jackson's tired army of fewer than four thousand men pitched into the Federals, which turned about to be a full reinforced division of about nine thousand. After a day of combat, Jackson's forces were defeated.

Jackson had just suffered his one and only tactical defeat; however, the battle turned out to be a tremendous strategic success. Convinced that Jackson would not have attacked unless he had a much larger army, the transfer of Banks's men was cancelled, and Banks's entire force reversed direction and marched back to the valley. Even worse from a Federal point of view, McDowell's entire corps was now stranded in place to protect to Washington. As a result, it was unable to play a significant role in either the Shenandoah Valley or the Richmond campaign. Banks, after returning to the valley, prepared to pursue Jackson once more.

Meanwhile, Jackson returned to Shenandoah County to reorganize his battered forces. Once again, Ashby, charged with protecting Jackson's rear, took up good defensive positions first at Cedar Creek and then at Hupp's Hill. Jackson continued south with the infantry and the wagon trains, making his headquarters at Schaffer's Hotel in Woodstock for a single day. The hotel

The Shenandoah County Courthouse. This stone courthouse was used by the contending armies throughout the war, and by the war's end, it was little more than a stone shell.

no longer stands, having been torn down and replaced by Shenandoah County's second courthouse.

Ashby stopped the Federal advance briefly at Woodstock when he shelled their advance. The Federals brought up several artillery pieces, which drove the Confederates away.

David Strother, a captain on Banks's staff, set up an office in the courthouse. When Banks visited the courthouse, he commented, "These quaint old buildings had turned out many strong men."

Regarding Woodstock, Strother said, "The place has a more cheerful aspect than Strasburg and seemed teeming with women and children who were all out to see us." Evidently, he did not care for the hotel, as he recorded in his journal, "The beds had been occupied by the Confederates the night before and dirty enough they were."

Jackson stopped at Narrow Passage, where he made his headquarters at the Stover home just south of Narrow Passage Creek. The Stover home, known at the time of the war as Willow Grove, still stands today,

The Inn at Narrow Passage was the Stover home in 1862. This house served as Jackson's headquarters for a brief time in 1862.

although it has been altered greatly in appearance. The old Stover home is now the upscale Inn at Narrow Passage. An important event happened during this time.

While at the Stover home, Jedediah Hotchkiss was called to meet with Jackson. In his journal, Hotchkiss recorded the events of that meeting:

> *March 26, 1862: In the morning our battalion was ordered back to Narrow Passage...near the rest of the army. Hd. Qrs. were established at Miss Stover's, in the stone house, near Narrow Passage Creek. Soon after we reached camp, Gen. Jackson sent me a message that he wished to see me. I promptly reported, when he said, after some general conversation about my topographical work in Northwestern Virginia last year, "I want you to make me a map of the Valley, from Harpers Ferry to Lexington, showing all the points of offence and defence in those places. Mr. Pendleton will give you orders for whatever outfit you want. Good morning, Sir."*

Thus was established one of the key participants in Jackson's future successes on the battlefield. Hotchkiss immediately began his assigned tasks and pointed out potential problems with Jackson's position at Narrow Passage. Hotchkiss advised Jackson to move the army farther south to Rude's Hill, which was an easier position to defend. He also recommended establishing a strong picket line at Stony. Hotchkiss's maps and advice proved to be invaluable to Jackson during his famous Valley Campaign of 1862. Following Jackson's death at Chancellorsville in 1863, Hotchkiss continued his cartographic duties, serving under Generals Richard S. Ewell, as well as Jubal A. Early. At least half of the Confederate maps published in the *Official Atlas of the Civil War* are attributed to him and his staff.

Jackson then moved on to Rude's Hill, where he established a camp for most of his infantry and the militia. While at Rude's Hill, Jackson's headquarters were in the residence of the Reverend A.R. Rude.

The Rude home is now a dilapidated house sitting at the foot of Rude's Hill, but it has a rich Civil War history. At the start of the war, this home, called Locust Grove, was owned by Reverend A.R. Rude, a retired Lutheran preacher and his wife, the widow of William Steenberger. Reverend Rude welcomed the Southerners to their home, and several members of Jackson's staff commented on their cordial welcome. Most of Jackson's staff slept in one room. A few had beds, but most slept on the floor. General Jackson had a room to himself. It was here that Jackson's staff enjoyed a brief period of

The A.R. Rude home near Rude's Hill. This home was the headquarters of General Jackson for two weeks in 1862.

relaxation and got a better chance to get to know one another. Hotchkiss described the scene:

> *We often had very pleasant times. The Adjutant General A.S. Pendleton is a grandson of the revolutionary Col. Pendleton and is a very fine young man, a gentleman in every way. The Medical Director, Dr. Hunter McGuire is a very smart fellow and gives us entertaining medical predilections at our evening sittings. Gen. Jackson is quite deaf; spends most of his time in his room, by himself, except when in the saddle; but he is very pleasant and I like him much.*

This was not the last time this historic old home would receive guests, some expected and some not. After his wife died, Reverend Rude moved to Texas, and the home was taken over by Reverend Addison Weller, another Lutheran minister. Federal major general David "Black Dave" Hunter used the home as a headquarters for a brief period in June 1864. After being mortally wounded in the area, the famous Confederate partisan ranger Captain John

Home at the Red Banks farm. The house, owned at the time by the Ripley family, was used by a number of Confederate officers during the war.

"Hanse" McNeill was taken to the house, where he was treated before dying in Harrisonburg. It is said by many local people that Federal general Philip Sheridan visited the home and may have spent one night there.

Rude's Hill became a favorite camping ground for the Confederates and was used repeatedly throughout the war. Jackson remained at Rude's Hill for over two weeks recruiting new soldiers, electing new company-grade officers and replacing all three of his brigade commanders.

While two of Jackson's brigades were located at Rude's Hill, the Stonewall Brigade camped at Camp Buchannan, located in the fields next to Red Banks. Brigadier General Richard B. Garnett was the commander of the Stonewall Brigade at the time of the Battle of Kernstown, and Jackson unjustly blamed Garnett for retreating from the battlefield without permission. Jackson went to Garnett's headquarters in the Red Banks home, arrested him and relieved him from command. Garnett was replaced by Brigadier General Charles S. Winder.

In September, General Lee ordered that the charges against Garnett be dropped, but damage to Garnett's reputation was done. Garnett became the commander of one of George Pickett's brigades and was killed at Gettysburg during the Pickett-Pettigrew Charge.

Winder had a richly deserved reputation as a strict disciplinarian and was widely resented by both the officers and men now under him. It was Winder who helped to convince Jackson to take stronger disciplinary action against soldiers who left the ranks without permission. He drilled his new brigade without mercy, and several of his men threatened to kill him during the next battle.

The young men who were not already in the army learned from newspapers that the Confederate Congress had adopted a military draft that would take effect on April 16. Those who voluntarily enlisted would receive a bounty and had a better chance of being assigned to a unit of their choosing. The news caused many young men to flock to Rude's Hill to join up. Because of a lack of available firearms, Richmond actually sent a shipment of pikes to Jackson, but there is no evidence that Jackson ever used these pikes.

To augment recruiting efforts, Governor Letcher ordered that state militias be disbanded and their members inducted into the ranks of the Confederate army. In what became known as the "Rockingham Rebellion," a number of Rockingham militiamen decided to resist enlistment, left the camps at Rude's Hill and took refuge in the Blue Ridge Mountains near Swift Run Gap. Jackson ordered Lieutenant Colonel John R. Jones of the Thirty-third Virginia, with a mixed force of infantry, cavalry and artillery, to quash the "rebellion." Jones performed his duties well, and within a few days most of the mutinous militiamen were arrested.

While Jackson was tending to his reorganization duties, Ashby was busy sparring with the Federals. From March 24 through the end of the month, the Confederate cavalry with Chew's artillery camped in and around the town of Woodstock, where the men of Chew's battery were quartered in the old courthouse. Banks's lethargic advance finally entered Woodstock on the first day of April, but not without a few parting shots from Confederate artillery. Private Neese recalled:

> We halted on the hill at the south end of town (Woodstock) a few minutes, then fell back to Narrow Passage. On the hill south of Narrow Passage we went into position and fired at the advancing enemy as it came into range. Their four-gun battery replied to our fire and we played ball with them a while with two guns to four.

With Banks's cavalry on his heels, Ashby reached Edinburg and took up good defensive positions on the opposite side of the Stony Creek. Ashby positioned Chew's artillery on Whissen Hill near the old cemetery on the bluff above Stony Creek. From there, he began shelling the approaching Federals. Banks answered by placing a Federal battalion on Academy or Schoolhouse Hill north of town. From those positions, the two sides fired at each other over the center of the town. Then, just as suddenly as it had appeared, the Confederate artillery limbered up and disappeared. Private Neese of Chew's battery left this account of that encounter:

> *Then* [we] *fell back to a hill a little south of Edenburg...The Yanks followed our retreat and put their battery in position on the hill at the north end of Edenburg...The firing was rapid for awhile, and right across the center of town. Our cavalry burned the railroad and pike bridge at Stony Creek...We fell back to Red Banks, eight miles from Woodstock on the north fork of the Shenandoah, and camped.*

Ashby's troops, along with several companies of infantry, set up a picket line along the far side of the creek. The Federals pushed forward their picket line into town but did not make any serious attempt to cross the creek in force. Banks seemed content to hold his position, with his advance resting on the creek and his rear stretching back to Woodstock. Ashby extended his picket line farther west and eventually all the way to Columbia Furnace. During the next two weeks, there were daily skirmishes between Confederate and Federal forces along the banks of Stony Creek. Ashby established his camp just below the crest of Pence's Hill near the creek. Although Jackson was primarily occupied with refitting his army, he coordinated closely with Ashby and shuffled infantry units back and forth from his camps at Red Banks and Rude's Hill to support Ashby's line.

Private John Worsham, a member of Company F, Twenty-first Virginia Infantry, described what he witnessed while at Edinburg during the period:

> *F Company was ordered forward as skirmishers through a Wood, halting on its edge. A large open field was in our front, and Edinburg in full view and the Yankee skirmish line on the opposite side of the creek. We engaged them at once. Col. Ashby came along, riding his white horse; he had the dwarf courier with him, and he told us not to fire unless the enemy attempted to cross the creek, and if they should make the attempt, to give it to them. He rode out in our front to a small hillock to see what was going on, the little courier accompanying him. The enemy immediately shot at them; as they reached the hillock, the courier's horse fell dead. We could hear*

Colonel Ashby tell him to take off his saddle, bridle and accouterments, and carry them to the rear, which he did a quickly as possible. Colonel A. sat his horse as quietly as if he had been in camp, until the courier reached the woods, when he quietly turned his horse and walked him off towards us, passing through our line going to the rear.

Banks took over Jackson's old headquarters at Willow Grove. While there, he requested cavalry, claiming the cavalry he had at hand was "weak in numbers and spirit." Washington dispatched seven companies from the First Vermont Cavalry under command of Colonel Jonas P. Holiday to Banks. Unfortunately for Banks, only a few days after their arrival at Strasburg, Colonel Holiday rode out along Tumbling Run and committed suicide by shooting himself. About that same time, Brigadier General John F. Hatch arrived to become Banks's chief of cavalry, and he seemed to have a positive effect on Banks's operations during this period.

Finally, on April 16, Banks, reinforced to the extent with which he was comfortable, prepared for his advance.

A company of Ashby's cavalry, the Brock's Gap Rifles, was assigned to picket the Columbia Furnace area. Columbia Furnace was a small village of about twenty-five houses, extensive furnace buildings, a large country store, a hotel and a large brick house in which furnace officials lived. A couple Union sympathizers brought information to the First Squadron of the Pennsylvania Cavalry about the location and strength of the Confederates based there. Using that information, a combined force of cavalry and infantry set out to capture the pickets.

Leaving their camp about midnight on April 17, the Federals did not have an easy time of it at first. It was drizzling rain, and the group got lost. Once they found the right route, they crept up to the two churches on a hill above the village where the Confederates were housed. It was just after daybreak, and the Confederate cooks were building fires to prepare breakfast. The Federals deployed and charged between the churches, yelling and firing as they advanced. Most of the Confederates were still asleep in a church, but when they awoke, they tried unsuccessfully to escape. The Federals captured three officers and about sixty troops, along with all their equipment and over seventy horses. This incident points out a criticism often made by General Jackson concerning General Ashby's discipline among his troops. Shortly after the capture of the Confederate pickets, Bank's entire army began a general advance across Stony Creek. General Shields's division crossed the ford at Columbia Furnace and marched up the Back Road, while Brigadier

General Nathan Kimball's division followed the Vermont cavalry up the Valley Pike.

Meanwhile, about midnight, the First Vermont Cavalry Regiment assembled along the Valley Pike north of Edinburg and prepared to move south. A historian for the regiment wrote after the war:

> At midnight the column moved forward, the Vermont cavalry in advance, under whispered commands, though the tramp of hoofs, and rumble of artillery must have announced to all around that a heavy force was in motion. Before daylight the skies in front reddened by the light of burning bridges, showed that the enemy was fully aware of the advance. At daybreak the head of the column passed through the lower village of Mount Jackson.

As the Vermonters reached the north end of Mount Jackson, they encountered Ashby's men, "busily engaged in firing the station houses and cars and the bridge across Mill Creek." Columns of smoke rose high over the area, and sparks floating in the breeze threatened the destruction of houses along the pike. After some preliminary artillery fire, Federal infantrymen began to filter around the town. The Vermonters received the order: "Make ready for a charge."

The Green Mountain Boys, as they were called, moved along at a trot through the northern end of town in columns of four. The sound of the artillery from both sides became more frequent. A bugle sounded the charge, and the Vermonters raced through the village. "With lifted sabres glistening in the morning sunlight, and clatter of thousands of hoofs on the hard turnpike, and clinging of scabbards...the long column dashed into the village."

The bridge over Mill Creek was in flames, but many of the Vermonters forded the stream and continued their pursuit of Ashby's rear guard almost to the north end of the bridge over the North Fork. Confederate artillery mounted on the crest of Rude's Hill prepared to fire.

Near Mount Jackson, the North Fork flows through a gorge with steep, rocky banks on both sides, making it a formidable obstacle if the bridge were destroyed. It is this topography around the bridge that made the location so important to both armies throughout much of the war.

Ashby waited at the bridge to ensure its destruction. The fuel was piled to fire it, but Ashby waiting until his rear guard cleared the town. What really happened next is difficult to determine. Several of the participants that day wrote about the fight at the North Fork bridge. Everyone agrees on

The abutments of the original bridge over the North Fork at Mount Jackson. This area was the scene of combat at least eight times during the Civil War.

the fact that General Ashby was almost captured near the bridge when his beautiful white horse was mortally wounded, but accounts vary greatly as to circumstances. The Federal cavalry reached the bridge and used the nose bags from their horses to gather water to extinguish the fire.

Confederate artillery on Rude's Hill delayed the Federal advance long enough to allow the withdrawal of the men and equipment from the hill. Jackson's proceeded to Harrisonburg and then turned southeast until he reached Swift Run Gap, where he went into camp.

In the meantime, Jackson's request for reinforcements was granted, and Richmond ordered Major General Richard E. Ewell with his division to join Jackson. As Ewell's division reached Swift Run Gap, he was shocked to see Jackson preparing to move again. Jackson left Ewell at Swift Run Gap to hold Banks in place while he took his smaller force and marched south through Brown's Gap to Mechum's Station on the Virginia Central Railroad. Jackson's move was designed to deceive Union major general John C. Frémont into thinking he was headed for Richmond. On May 3, Jackson bivouacked at Mechum's Station.

Even Jackson's own men thought they were headed to Richmond. The next day, when trains arrived, the troops were elated to find they were headed for Staunton and not Richmond. After arriving at Staunton, Jackson moved west, united with General Edward Johnson's troops and marched against part of Frémont's army at McDowell in Highland County. At the Battle of McDowell on May 8, Jackson defeated the advance of Frémont's army under Brigadier General Robert H. Milroy and Brigadier General Robert C. Schenck. Thus began Jackson's 1862 Shenandoah Valley Campaign.

On May 4, 1862, Banks, convinced that Jackson had gone to Richmond, withdrew to New Market. On May 12, Shields's division was detached from Banks and marched east through New Market Gap, leaving Banks with only eight thousand men. Banks fell back to Woodstock and then to Strasburg, where he went into his prepared works. The centerpiece of Banks's field works was a large earthen fort located on a hill overlooking Strasburg.

The fort was almost complete, although heavy artillery had yet to be mounted. Edward B. Hunt, a captain of engineers, had selected the position and supervised the construction of the fort. Hunt, having examined defensive positions in the valley, had reported his findings to Banks in a dispatch recommending the construction at Strasburg. He gave his reasons and a description of the fort in his dispatch of April 10, 1862:

> *The hill north of Strasburg has so effective a command over the roads, the railroad, and town, and would afford so much security to a depot of supplies, &c., at Strasburg, that I have staked out the lines of a field fort on it, and have indicated to Captain Mason and to Mr. Douglass (who is engaged to report to you for its construction) all the essentials for making it what is needed. By peculiar arrangement of a grand traverse the command by the surrounding hills will be made mostly ineffective.*

At this time, Captain Elijah "Lige" White commanded an independent cavalry company from Loudoun County known as White's Rebels. The company, assigned to General Ewell's division, was given the task of reporting the progress of Federal fortifications at Strasburg. White's men watched the Federals in Strasburg from Three-Top Mountain. The rough trail to the mountaintop could only be reached through Fort Valley. It was at this time that Captain White received the first of many wounds he suffered during the war. Descending the mountain, White received information from a Confederate sympathizer that two Yankees were at a neighbor's house. White quickly captured two Yankees, along with their horses, and continued

View of Fisher's Hill and the Massanuttens taken from the remains of Banks Fort in Strasburg.

on to their camp when they ran into local bushwhackers. Thinking the intruders were Yankees, White and his men opened fire, wounding one man. The bushwhackers retuned fire, and White was wounded in the face. His wounds were serious but not fatal. He was treated by a local doctor and was taken later to Charlottesville to recuperate.

During his stay in Strasburg, a Federal chaplain reported the place to be the "dirtiest, nastiest, meanest, poorest, most shiftless town I have ever seen in all the shiftless, poor, mean, nasty, dirty towns of this beautiful valley." Because of its proximity to the fort, St. Paul's Lutheran Church was ransacked, gutted and converted into an arsenal. The pews of the church were used to make soldiers' coffins. Sometime later, the Federals converted the church building into a stable for their horses. A number of the homes and churches had been converted into hospitals for those Federals who became ill.

Following his victory at McDowell, Jackson followed the departing Federals for several days and then prepared to return to the valley after coordinating with Ewell at Mount Solon. Jackson moved to Harrisonburg, where he began a rapid march down the pike designed to create the impression that he was about to attack Strasburg from the south. When Jackson reached New Market, he sent part of Ashby's cavalry under Major Samuel Myers on to Fisher's Hill to screen his true movement and enhance the perception of an attack on Banks's front. At New Market, Jackson turned unexpectedly east, crossed the Massanuttens and joined forces with Ewell at Luray. On May 23, Jackson's combined force descended on the Federal garrison at Front Royal, effectively eliminating it. Once more splitting his force, Jackson advanced along two routes toward Winchester, threatening to cut off Banks's forces around Strasburg. When Banks was alerted to the disaster at Front Royal, he realized that Jackson was about to be in his rear.

Banks quickly prepared for a race to Winchester, assigning Colonel Othneil de Forest and the Fifth New York Cavalry to form the rear guard. Before leaving town, Forest destroyed part of the supplies stockpiled at Strasburg. Forest later reported:

> *Halting my command at the south end of the village, I emptied the church of the ordnance stores and burned them, and then partly emptied the freight depot after loading a supply train of 13 wagons with clothing; but being pressed for time, I finally fired the depot, as well as a large outbuilding to the south.*

Jackson, moving from Cedarville to Middletown, reached the Valley Pike only after the majority of Banks's troops had already passed. Unsure where to find Banks, Jackson sent Ashby's cavalry north while Jackson, with his infantry, headed to Strasburg. Jackson soon found that the small force in his front at Hupp's Hill was Forest with the rear guard. Forest continued:

> *I found that my own command, as well as a portion of the First Vermont Cavalry, a portion of General Banks' bodyguard, and Hampton's battery were cut off from the main body by the rebels. Infantry, cavalry, and wagons were streaming back in wild confusion along the road and the fields on either side as far as the eye could reach.*

Forest retreated back to Strasburg and escaped to the west along the Capon Grade. Jackson quickly reversed his direction and moved toward Winchester. In a skillful attack, Jackson won the Battle of Winchester on May 25. Banks retreated to Martinsburg and crossed the Potomac at Williamsport on May 26.

During the three-day fight, Jackson's army captured at least 2,100 men. Equally important, Jackson's men seized thousands of badly needed small arms and ammunition; tons of food, including delicacies from sutlers' wagons; good-quality medical stores; and brand-new uniforms and accoutrements. The Southerners began to refer to the defeated Federal general as "Commissary Banks." So many Confederates began wearing captured blue uniforms that Jackson had to outlaw the practice.

Jackson had succeeded in preventing reinforcements from being sent to McDowell, but now he had to survive the coming Federal response. Lincoln was determined to trap Jackson or at least cut off his supplies. Despite objections from McDowell and McClellan, who surmised the real purpose of Jackson's operations, Lincoln and Stanton demanded an end to Jackson's devilment. Lincoln ordered McDowell's corps, which had already begun its advance toward Richmond, to stop and proceed west through Front Royal to Strasburg. Frémont was supposed to move east from his position and take Harrisonburg, thereby putting him in Jackson's rear, but he was stopped by a small Confederate force in the passes west of Harrisonburg. Rather than attack them, Frémont marched forty miles north and crossed into the valley near Strasburg.

Shields's division spearheaded the march of McDowell's corps and seized Front Royal from the Confederate troops garrisoned there. He then proceeded toward Strasburg. Frémont's army slowly wound its way to Lebanon Church, where a halt was called for the evening. Skirmishers were sent forward to Capon Grade, and headquarters were established at the Daniel Funkhouser home. Ashby sent several companies to watch Frémont as Jackson approached Strasburg.

Jackson's retreating army stretched for many miles along the Valley Pike. The immense train of wagons rolling along in columns of two hauling captured supplies and equipment led the column. Following were a large group of prisoners and the headquarters wagons. Two infantry brigades of Jackson's Valley Army and Ewell's division brought up the rear. As night fell, the main portion of the infantry slept on the north bank of Cedar Creek, while the wagon train continued through the night toward New Market. Jackson and his staff spent the night in the Hupp home. Winder's brigade, underway from Harpers Ferry, marched approximately twenty-five miles and halted near Newtown to allow stragglers to catch up before resuming the march at "first light."

Early the next morning, Jackson sent Ewell's troops to deal with Frémont's approach from the west. Ewell encountered Frémont's skirmishers and pickets along the Capon Grade and easily pushed them beyond the village of Clary by 10:00 a.m.

Fremont's initial positions

Early's initial position

Modern photograph of the battlefield near Clary where General Ewell's Confederates stopped the progress of General Frémont.

At noon, Winder's brigade finally reached Strasburg, where Winder allowed the men to sleep for several hours. They resumed the march at dusk, and Ewell withdrew from his contact with Frémont and followed Winder south to near Woodstock. By noon on June 1, Jackson's entire force had cleared Strasburg. Parts of three Federal armies with fifty thousand men had failed. Jackson escaped!

The First New Jersey Cavalry and the First Pennsylvania Cavalry cleared the Confederate rear guard out of Strasburg, capturing forty prisoners in town. Quickly, they turned south along the Valley Pike in pursuit of the retreating Confederates. Near Tom's Brook, they encountered the first serious resistance. Ashby placed his artillery on a hill commanding the pike. New Jersey troopers dismounted and sent out skirmish lines into the woods on both sides of the pike. Ashby had rallied Confederate stragglers to add to his own cavalry. A heavy fire from both sides continued for some time, until a six-gun battery of Federal artillery came up. The New Jersey skirmishers pushed forward so far that the Federal artillery shells began to fall among them. As more Federal horsemen arrived, they extended their skirmish lines until they threatened to overlap Ashby's position. Ashby retired to another hilltop position, again slowing the Federal pursuit.

At Woodstock, Jackson made headquarters at the courthouse and surrounding buildings in Lawyers' Row. From the captured sutlers' stores, the weary staff, reported Kyd Douglas, feasted on "a sumptuous table: cake and pickled lobsters, cheese, canned peaches, piccolomini and candy, coffee, ale, and condensed milk. It was a feast the like of which was seldom vouchsafed to Confederate soldiers, and with inexpressible thanks we drank the health of General Banks." Many scholars believe it was here that Jackson informed Ashby of his promotion to brigadier general.

Back in Strasburg, the Federals came to grips with the fact that Jackson was gone. It was quickly agreed that Frémont would follow the Confederates up the Valley Pike while Shields returned to Front Royal and marched up the Page Valley in an attempt to get on Jackson's flank.

On June 2, near Woodstock, Ashby encountered a sizable force of Brigadier General George Bayard's cavalry backed by infantry and artillery. This time, Ashby's forces were accompanied by Brigadier General George H. "Maryland" Steuart, in command of the Second Virginia and the Sixth Virginia Cavalry. The Confederates deployed with each command forming on one side of the Valley Pike. Bayard's men charged Steuart's side of the line, and when the two forces met, there was a general mêlée, with confusion gripping Steuart. Steuart, an incompetent cavalry commander, mismanaged his part in the affair by ordering the Second to fire into an infantry formation he believed was the enemy. As it turned out, it was the Twenty-seventh Virginia Infantry. Further confusion erupted when the Second Virginia Cavalry broke and stampeded into the lines of the Forty-eighth Virginia Infantry. Lieutenant Colonel Thomas Garnett of the Forty-eighth Infantry wrote that the charge on the Second Cavalry caused "a most disgraceful retreat." The Forty-eighth regrouped and, aided by the Forty-second Virginia Infantry, halted the stampede and protected the retreat of the Confederate troops.

Several days later, Colonels Thomas Flournoy and Thomas T. Munford went to General Ewell and requested that their regiments, the Sixth and Second Virginia Cavalry, be transferred to the command of Turner Ashby, recently promoted to brigadier general. Ewell agreed and went to Jackson for final approval. Jackson gave his consent, and for the remainder of the war, Steuart would serve as an infantry commander.

At Woodstock, Bayard's cavalry was able to recapture a number of the men it lost in skirmishes over the last several days. It then took up the pursuit, although its quarry was no longer in sight.

It continued to rain throughout the day, and Jackson, at the insistence of his staff, agreed to stop again at the Allen home in Hawkinstown. Colonel George Patton, in command of the infantry part of the rear guard, stopped at the Allen home to speak with Jackson. Jackson was irritated at the success the Federal cavalry was having and asked Patton for an explanation. Patton gave an explanation, ending with a comment about the bravery of the three officers who led a charge and how he hated to see his men fire at them. Jackson's reply was: "Shoot them, Colonel. I don't want them to be so brave."

From Rude's Hill, Jackson retired on June 3 to the vicinity of New Market. This time, Ashby was successful in his efforts to burn the bridge over the North Fork south of Mount Jackson. Frémont quickly laid a pontoon bridge across the river, but the rapidly moving river broke it and delayed his advance for yet another day. This day gave Jackson the time he needed. He was able to save his entire command and most of his captured property. While at Mount Jackson, Frémont's Federals converted the Graham Hotel into a U.S. General Hospital.

The Central Hotel in Mount Jackson, now an apartment building. At the time of the war, this hotel was owned by Michael Graham and was used as a Federal hospital.

By June 5, Jackson's army had reached Harrisonburg, where it turned east toward Port Republic. In another severe rear guard action near Harrisonburg on June 6, General Turner Ashby was killed while leading a charge against the Federals.

Frémont's troops advanced up the Valley Turnpike while Shields's column marched up the Luray Road along the South Fork. Jackson left Ewell's division at Cross Keys to hold Frémont at bay while he concentrated his forces near the bridge at Port Republic. Ewell drove Frémont back, keeping him from crossing the South Fork, and the following day, Jackson and Ewell defeated Shields's advance. Both Union forces retreated, freeing Jackson's army to reinforce the Confederate army at Richmond.

Jackson's campaign accomplished the relief of pressure against Richmond that Lee had hoped for. In five weeks, Jackson's army had marched more than 650 miles and inflicted more than 7,000 casualties, at a cost of only 2,500. More importantly, Jackson's campaign had tied up Union forces three times his strength. Jackson's victories infused new hope and enthusiasm for the Confederate cause and materially contributed to the defeat of McClellan's campaign against Richmond.

On June 12, Frémont's retiring army went into camp at New Market and Mount Jackson. Continuing his withdrawal, he halted at Woodstock on June 19 and at Strasburg the following day. On June 26, Lincoln consolidated the three forces of Frémont, Banks and McDowell into a new Army of Virginia, commanded by Major General John Pope. This action so irked Frémont that he resigned. By mid-July, Pope had withdrawn his command to the east side of the Blue Ridge.

Following Ashby's death, sixteen of the twenty-six companies now in the Seventh Virginia Cavalry were reorganized into the Twelfth Virginia Cavalry and the Seventeenth Battalion Virginia Cavalry. A new cavalry brigade was formed consisting of the Sixth, Seventh and Twelfth Regiments; the Seventeenth Battalion; and Colonel Preston Chew's Horse Artillery, to be commanded by Brigadier General Beverly Robertson.

When Pope withdrew the Federal forces from the valley, Robertson's cavalry brigade received orders to join Jackson near Richmond, leaving only Companies B and K of the Twelfth Cavalry behind to guard the lower valley. Company B was located near Harrisonburg, with Company K stationed at Mount Jackson. These two detached companies served as pickets during the balance of 1862, while major military operations were conducted elsewhere.

After defeating two armies on the soil of Virginia, General Lee crossed the Potomac River and invaded Maryland. On September 17, his men clashed with a Federal army under McClellan near the town of Sharpsburg. The one-day battle that followed was the bloodiest day in American military history. Although outnumbered two to one, Lee battled McClellan's army to a standstill. In one day's fighting, the two armies suffered a combined total of more than twenty-three thousand casualties. Following the battle, Lee ordered the battered Army of Northern Virginia to withdraw across the Potomac to the safety of the Shenandoah Valley. The Confederate retreat was preceded by an immense wagon train carrying thousands of wounded. Once again, the homes and hospitals of Shenandoah County received many of the wounded who could not be treated in Winchester. Local citizens gathered once more at the telegraph office to wait for the casualty lists to be delivered.

The entire Confederate army rested north of Winchester for several weeks following Antietam. Visitors from the area traveled back and forth with packages of clothing and edibles for their friends and relatives in the army. Many county soldiers were allowed leave to go home to visit their families and help with the harvest. Then, in late October, Lee moved with Longstreet's corps over the Blue Ridge to establish a new line near Culpeper Court House. On November 23, 1862, Jackson received orders to join Lee at Fredericksburg. The following day, Jackson began the withdrawal that would take him from the valley for the last time. On the twenty-fourth and twenty-fifth, the valley army trudged through Shenandoah County and marched east to join Lee.

Robertson's cavalry brigade, now under the command of Brigadier General W.E. "Grumble" Jones, withdrew from above Winchester to a more secure area around New Market. From there, the brigade kept a close watch on any Federal attempts to reoccupy the lower valley. On December 21, Brigadier General Cluseret led a force east from Wardensville toward Strasburg; however, the troopers from Jones's brigade drove him back to their base. General Jones's cavalry established winter quarters in the valley with the Seventh Virginia Cavalry under Colonel R.H. Dulaney camped near Mount Jackson; the Eleventh Virginia Cavalry under Colonel O.R. Funsten camped near Edinburg; and the First Maryland Battalion under Major Ridgely Brown camped at New Market. Companies from these units were deployed on picket duty at various strategic points throughout the county.

THE YEAR 1863

Brigadier General Robert Huston Milroy, an ardent abolitionist, reoccupied Winchester on January 1, 1863. Milroy saw himself as a crusader who was sent to free the slaves. The weather was not conducive to prolonged military activity, so Milroy contented himself with making the Winchester secessionists suffer his wrath. On February 26, Captain F.A. Bond, with about sixty Maryland troopers, left his post at Strasburg and traveled by the Cedar Creek Grade to Kernstown, where he attacked a group of about fifteen Federal pickets. The Federals were warming themselves in a house when the Confederates attacked. Several Federals were killed, and seven others were captured, along with nine horses. The Marylanders headed back to Strasburg without losing a man.

Upon learning of the attack, Milroy quickly sent out five hundred troopers from the Thirteenth Pennsylvania Cavalry Regiment in hot pursuit over the frozen valley pike. Moving quickly, the Federals almost caught the retreating Confederates, but Bond managed to escape. The Federal column reached the main post of Jones's pickets (Companies A and D, First Maryland Cavalry) camped on Strawberry Hill on Fisher's Hill and chased them for some distance beyond Woodstock. During the chase, the Federals managed to recapture their own men, along with eleven Confederates. The Federals then split into two columns, some pursuing the fleeing pickets along the Back Road, while others continued down the Valley Pike attempting to capture a Confederate wagon train carrying forage. A group of Maryland infantrymen camped in the area repelled the Federal attack on the wagons.

When word of the skirmish reached Jones's headquarters in Edinburg, the general ordered the Eleventh Regiment to move to the action. About two miles from Woodstock, Funsten and 120 men met General Jones, who told him the Federals were just ahead in vastly superior numbers. Jones ordered a charge in any event.

Jones and Funsten rushed past the Federal rear guard that occupied the high ground near the pike and charged the rear of the Federal column. The surprised Federals fled, and attempts by their officers to rally the men were unsuccessful. Here is how the fight continued, according to Colonel Funsten:

> We pressed them hotly, using both saber and revolver with good effect, to Cedar Creek Bridge, a distance of about 12 miles, where part of them made a stand. I halted the front of the column to close up preparatory to renewing the charge, my command being greatly reduced by the capture and

guarding of prisoners, of whom the number already taken was greater than that with which I made the attack.

At this time, Colonel Dulany arrived with about 220 men from the Seventh Regiment. The Seventh then took up the fight and completed the victory. According to Dulany's report, the battle went this way:

When we reached the high ground beyond Strasburg we found the enemy had retired and again formed about 300 yards south of Cedar Creek. About 130 had crossed the Creek and…about 250 had formed to meet us. As we came in sight of each other, they seemed to advance slowly toward us, but when we got within 200 yards, our sabers drawn and the charge ordered, their hearts failed them, and wheeling in beautiful order, they went at full speed to the bridge, crossed, and again formed to receive us. As but 2 men would cross the bridge abreast, they could easily have prevented our crossing with their long-range guns, as their position was very strong and higher than the bridge. Changing the direction of our column we crossed the creek at the ford some 200 yards below the bridge. As soon as part of my command had crossed, the enemy again broke, not waiting for us to close with them. They having rested their horses some ten minutes…we could not overtake them until near Middletown. The race now became truly exciting…the fastest horses in our column taking the lead. As we came up with the rear, not a man that I saw offered to surrender until driven back by the sabers of my men or shot. Some, finding we were overtaking them, slipped from their horses and sought refuge in the houses along the road, and many had thrown their pistols away when captured.

Several miles beyond Middletown, Dulany ordered a halt, as the horses were totally worn out from a run of more than twenty-six miles. According to Jones's report of this action, about two hundred Federal cavalrymen, along with their horses and equipment, were captured. A number of others were killed or wounded in the action. Milroy said of the incident: "The conduct of our cavalry was disgraceful and cowardly."

When the weather improved, Milroy became more aggressive. On April 22, 1863, he sent a combined force of infantry, cavalry and artillery, under the command of Federal brigadier general Washington L. Elliott, on a scouting mission into Shenandoah County. As part of this mission, Colonel James A. Gallagher of the Thirteenth Pennsylvania Cavalry led his troopers through Strasburg to ascertain the strength of the Confederate outpost at the Strawberry Hill camp. Major Samuel Myers was in command of the Strawberry Hill post. His command consisted of one full cavalry company, along with approximately fifty dismounted cavalrymen known as Company Q. Myers decided to try to ambush the unsuspecting Federals. Myers concealed his dismounted troopers just east of the pike and thirty or forty yards off the road. Once the ambush was set, Myers, along with several mounted troopers, rode out onto the pike to within sight of the Federals near Spengler's Mill.

The Federal advance immediately gave chase as Myers retreated back past the point where the dismounted troopers were hidden. The Federals were nearly two-thirds of the way past the concealed position when the hidden Confederates rose and fired a volley. The pike was immediately "transformed into a sea of scrambling men and horses":

> *Confusion reigned supreme, and the enemy fled, panic-stricken with none to rally and none willing to be rallied. The spoils of victory were rapidly gathered up, consisting of some forty army revolvers, twenty-five carbines thirty sabres, and eighteen horses. The dead and wounded amounted to at least forty, which, together with some fifteen prisoners, made an aggregate of fifty-five, a man of the enemy for every one engaged on our side. The despatch [sic] sent by Major Myers to Colonel Funsten, after giving the result, concluded thus: "Glorious for Company Q; she gave the enemy fits today.*

General Elliott shelled the ambush area and sent infantry out only to discover that the Confederates were gone. Having no success, he retired toward Winchester. As soon as he withdrew, Major Myers and his small command reoccupied the picket line at Fisher's Hill.

Although accounts vary as to the extent of the casualties suffered by the Thirteenth Pennsylvania (between twenty-seven and seventy), the ambush was successful, and many new mounts were secured for service in the Confederate cavalry.

Between April 24 and May 22, 1863, Confederate cavalry under Generals William E. "Grumble" Jones and John D. Imboden conducted a successful raid into north-central West Virginia. Their goals were to disrupt the B&O Railroad and gather cattle and other supplies. The raiders covered seven hundred miles and fought two battles and several skirmishes. Along the way, they captured nearly seven hundred prisoners, 1,000 cattle and 1,200 horses. They burned an oil facility along with sixteen railroad bridges.

On the main Virginia battle front, Federal troops suffered stinging defeats at Fredericksburg in December 1862 and Chancellorsville in May 1863. In both cases, the Union army suffered humiliating losses and thousands of casualties, but in neither case was the Federal army destroyed. Both victories had also been very costly to the South. The loss of officers and men was immense, including Jackson, who was mortally wounded on the evening of May 2. The losses in the valley regiments were so great that a special edition of the *Rockingham Register* was printed giving lists of the casualties. Following the death of Jackson, Lee reorganized his army into three corps. The valley regiments now fell under the command of Major General Richard S. Ewell.

War on the Homefront

The demand for farm produce by the Richmond government stripped the county of most of its stored grain and meat. Herds were thinned, and the demand for hogs outstripped farmers' ability to replace them. With the men away at the front, families feared that many of their fertile fields would not be plowed and planted in the spring. The people of the valley were learning to make do with less and, in some cases, make substitutions for commodities impossible to find as the Federal blockade tightened its grip. Salt continued to be in short supply, and Shenandoah County had difficulty finding horse teams and wagons to haul its allotment the 160 miles from the Saltville mines in Smyth and Washington Counties.

Support for the war was further dividing the population. Some ardent supporters waved their flags and carried on while others began to doubt the value of continuing the war. A few families encouraged their sons to take refuge with relatives in loyal states to avoid conscription. Others hid at home or in the mountains and took their chances against being caught and impressed into service. Conscript details, always one facet of the Confederate army following the adoption of the first draft law, increased substantially in 1863. These details roamed through the county to arrest and return absentees to their respective commands. This duty was not welcomed by most because it often involved taking former friends from their families to face courts-martial for desertion. Despite the shortages and all the deaths of Shenandoah County men over the last year, most residents still believed the war would be over in the coming year and the Confederacy would be left alone to peruse its own destiny.

THE GETTYSBURG CAMPAIGN

In the late spring, Jones's Brigade was recalled from the valley to join Jeb Stuart and most of the other cavalry near Brandy Station. Before leaving the valley, the brigade was reviewed by Brigadier General Albert G. Jenkins near Fisher's Hill. Stuart, preparing for the coming invasion of Pennsylvania, held a grand review for Robert E. Lee on June 8, 1863, just outside the town of Culpeper. The following day, the Union cavalry corps launched a surprise attack on Stuart's cavalry. After an all-day fight in which fortunes changed repeatedly, the Federals retired. From this point in the war, the Federal cavalry gained strength and confidence. Brandy Station was the largest cavalry battle of the war and the opening engagement of the Gettysburg campaign.

The Battle of Gettysburg was a disaster for the Confederate army. During the battle and the subsequent retreat, the Confederates suffered 4,708 men killed and another 12,693 wounded and 5,830 captured. The Confederates started back toward Virginia with a wagon train some seventeen miles in length. They reached the rain-swollen Potomac River at Williamsport on July 6, but many could not recross until the fourteenth. During the second week of July, four thousand Federal prisoners captured around Gettysburg began the march through the county along Valley Pike under guard by Imboden's cavalry. They shuffled through Strasburg and stopped for the night south of town. On July 14, they passed through Woodstock and Edinburg and camped about seven miles north of Mount Jackson. They reached Harrisonburg on July 16.

During this same period, Lee's sick and wounded also began their hundred-mile trek from Winchester to the General and Receiving Hospital at Staunton. The more seriously wounded and those too sick to move on foot were hauled in wagons without springs, their only padding being some straw on the wagon floor. Those who could walk were forced to do so. The journey took them through Strasburg, Edinburg, Woodstock, Mount Jackson, New Market and Harrisonburg. Mount Jackson was the site of the first wayside hospital south of Winchester. Most of those who could not complete the long journey were unloaded at Mount Jackson Hospital or at other locations where treatment could be found. (The treatment of the casualties is discussed more fully in chapter six.)

The people living along the turnpike tried to alleviate the suffering as much as they could. As in the lower valley, private homes and taverns were opened to the sick and wounded soldiers who passed by. A reporter for the *Richmond Sentinel* wrote:

Federals Invade the County

At Harrisonburg and New Market, systematic arrangements were made for feeding the hungry; men being stationed near the road to hail them as they passed and supply them, without charge, with what they needed, while volunteer physicians and kindhearted ladies were at hand to give such relief to their wounds as a mere passing attention would secure...the endless ambulance trains, accompanied by hobbling sick and wounded soldiers, began streaming into Harrisonburg on 9 July. "Nothing but poor distressed soldiers," wrote one citizen, "passed through the town for nearly two full weeks."

On July 25, Lieutenant Robert Funkhouser of the Forty-ninth Virginia Infantry made an entry in his diary:

The whole train is crowded with lame men. Pass through Edinburg, through Mount Jackson where our sick and wounded from Winchester, etc. were being delivered. By this time nearly half of the division had fallen out of ranks unable to keep up, officers as well as men.

During this same period, Cornelia Peake McDonald made notes in her journal about traveling on the Valley Turnpike during this period. She wrote that the road was

something to be avoided. It had originally been a beautiful macadam turnpike, but three years of heavy traffic of both armies had cut through the road metal until it was impassable. So the wagons, cannon, caissons, cavalry, and foot soldiers made roads on either side, and as soon as they got too bad, new ones were made. We passed many wagons which had been left stalled and many rotting corpses of horses and mules...Not a fence was to be seen for miles. No fields were planted, no farming going on in the richest piece of ground in the world. Part of the army were in front of us and more followed, and we were constantly in sight of, and often jostled by moving crowds of people and vehicles. Many wounded men were among them, making their way to a place of safety, while fugitives of every grade and degree were toiling on, on foot or in any kind of broken-down vehicle. Sick men, hungry men, and women with crowds of children, all hurrying on. One man I saw lying dead by the roadside. He had lain down to rest, and never rose again.

Soon it became necessary for Lee's army to leave the valley and move east to thwart another Federal advance. Many of the valley men passed their homes as they headed south on the Valley Pike to New Market, where they turned east toward Madison County and the line of the Rapidan and Rappahannock Rivers. The great armies had moved east, but death and destruction were far from over. Washington kept large contingents of Federals throughout the West Virginia counties that bordered Shenandoah Valley. Raids into Shenandoah County increased during the latter part of the year. Between September 19 and the 21, a detachment from the First New York Cavalry swept up the Valley Pike and entered Strasburg, capturing eleven Confederate cavalrymen, along with their horses and equipment. After scavenging about the town for two days, they tangled with some Confederates at Fisher's Hill before returning to their camp.

On November 15, 1863, Colonel William H. Boyd, commanding a seven-hundred-man mixed force, departed Charles Town for the lower valley. By evening, they had reached Strasburg and camped for the night. At dawn on the sixteenth, they broke camp and pressed on, reaching Woodstock by midmorning. Once again, the Yankees were in town. The Confederate pickets on duty made a feeble attempt to hold their position, but the odds were overwhelming, and the Confederates escaped to the south. As usual when the Federals came around, they checked the town for useful information and whatever they might pick up for personal use. In 1862, when Banks first came through Woodstock, there was plenty of good stuff to plunder. Now the stores were mostly empty, and private homes were still mostly off limits to theft. A sharp skirmish resulted in several Confederate pickets being driven from the town. The Federals captured a Southern officer, the mail carrier and several wagons, one of which was driven by Sergeant George Hamman of the Tenth Virginia Infantry. Hamman, recuperating from a wound received at Gettysburg, was hauling four barrels of apple brandy to Imboden's camp farther south.

Boyd's troopers moved on south to Edinburg, where they ran into another small group of Confederates who stood and fought for a short time before retiring. A few miles south of Edinburg, the Rebels made another brief stand in a piece of woods but were driven away when the Federals charged with sabers drawn. A few of the Union cavalrymen struck out after the fleeing Southerners but bit off more than they had bargained for. The Confederates saw that these cavalrymen were unsupported, so they stood and fought. As a result, three Federals were captured and another killed.

The Federals regrouped and resumed their ride south until they came within a mile of Mount Jackson. There they encountered Major Robert

White and the Forty-first Cavalry Battalion, along with a few men from Gilmor's command and a section of artillery posted on a slight hill. Boyd formed a line of battle on both sides of the pike and brought up his own artillery. After a few shells were fired into the town, the Confederates retreated. Boyd's men rushed through the town and across the bridge at Mill Creek, where they were again halted by the Confederates who occupied a hill just beyond.

The Union men drove the Confederates from this hill also but were again halted by White's men, who moved on to Rude's Hill on the other side of Meem's Bottom. The two sides watched each other for some time with little action taking place. Boyd saw that the Confederate artillery was positioned to be able to sweep the bridge over the North Fork, and he knew that the riverbank was too steep to allow his men to ford the river. Boyd also learned that he was opposed by nearly eight hundred Confederates, so he decided "it prudent not to pursue them any further." Boyd then retired back down the valley to Woodstock. As Boyd retired, he rounded up about one hundred head of cattle to take with him. Charles Moore, an ardent Union man, presented a pass to Boyd that had been signed by Banks and Frémont in an attempt to save the part of the herd that belonged to him, but his appeal fell on deaf ears. Such was the life of the unionist at that time.

During the night, Captain Davis, with about sixty Confederate cavalrymen, crept up on Boyd's camp and fired on it. Boyd, not knowing the size of the Rebel force, began a hasty retreat back toward Winchester. Somewhere along the Valley Pike, Boyd camped for the night. Early the next morning, as Boyd resumed his march, his men were fired on from a nearby house. A search of the house disclosed four of Harry Gilmor's men hiding beneath the floor. Incensed by this cowardly act, Boyd made his new prisoners walk to camp barefoot.

On December 7, one hundred troopers from the Twentieth Pennsylvania Cavalry commanded by Captain Theodore Singiser rode east from their camp at Springfield, West Virginia, with a mission to destroy Columbia Furnace. Columbia Furnace was a major supplier of iron to the Tredegar Ironworks in Richmond. Singiser proceeded through Wardensville and into the valley near Columbia Furnace. Confederate cavalry pickets stationed along Singiser's route were useless at either slowing his progress or alerting the guard at the furnace of his approach. Singiser troopers completely surprised the guards at the furnace, who quickly surrendered after a brief fight.

Singiser's trooper quickly set fire to the wooden structures and took other means to render the iron-making equipment inoperable. In a very short while,

The Irvin home at Columbia Furnace. This house was used by the manager of Columbia Furnace at the time of the war.

he paroled the captured vedettes and began his escape over to the Valley Pike at Woodstock. At Woodstock, he brushed aside a Confederate picket and cut the telegraph wires. He continued through Strasburg to Winchester. From there, he returned to his camp in West Virginia. Fortunately for the Confederacy, Singiser's efforts only stopped production at the furnace for a short time. Repairs were quickly made, and the production was resumed early in 1864. Two more attacks were made on the furnace before production permanently stopped near the end of the war.

Just as Singiser was completing his mission, Colonel George Wells was beginning another. Wells was assigned to command a combined force of infantry, artillery and cavalry totaling more than 1,100 men whose assignment was the destruction of the Virginia and Tennessee Railroad at Salem in Roanoke County. Wells left Charles Town on December 10 with a tight schedule to meet in order to disguise the true purpose of his mission.

Only days after Singiser's Yankees departed, the citizens of Strasburg were treated to a visit, this time from Wells. It was a cold, rainy day when Wells's Federals trotted into town and dispatched the few skirmishers left there. Wells was on an important mission, so he wasted little time before moving on, on December 18, to Woodstock, where he captured almost two dozen prisoners.

Opposing Wells's advance was a newly formed battalion commanded by Major Charles O'Ferrall, who would later become the governor of Virginia. Leaving the major part of his command several miles in his rear, O'Ferrall took about fifty men to slow the Federal advance, but without the assistance of artillery, he had little chance of stopping them. O'Ferrall watched the Federals move along the Valley Pike and skirmished with the advance whenever the opportunity presented itself. In his report of the affair, Colonel Wells claimed to have captured most of O'Ferrall's battalion, but O'Ferrall claimed to have harassed Wells so effectively as to cause the Federals to spend an entire day traveling the short distance between Edinburg and New Market.

While O'Ferrall was skirmishing with Wells, Major Harry Gilmor's troopers were operating in Fort Valley to protect the iron furnaces. Upon learning about the Federals in the area, Gilmor moved south through Fort Valley to wait for the Federals to pass so he could attack Wells's flank. On the way, he stopped and put rough shoes on his horses because the roads were icy. For two days, Gilmor and his men lay in the icy rain of the forest and then decided to make a stop at Burner's Springs, where they could find shelter and food. On the way, they had to swim through the partially frozen Passage Creek. Gilmor's scout reported that the resort was filled with refugees from other valley towns, and there were no accommodations available.

Not willing to spend another night in a frozen blanket, Gilmor had ten of his men don blue overcoats and move near Burner's Springs, where the people could easily see them. Just as Gilmor suspected, when they came into sight of the resort and prepared to charge, the guests took one look and immediately ran for the mountain nearby. Gilmor then brought in his men, spent a comfortable night and moved out the next morning. During the evening, Gilmor gave each of his men half a pint of brandy to keep them from catching cold. Gilmor said, "Strange to say, none of them did after lying out two days and nights in sleet and rain, in wet, frozen blankets, besides swimming a creek filled with ice."

When Gilmor left the fort, he learned that Wells had left a strong guard on the bridge that crossed the North Fork just south of Mount Jackson. Once again, the bridge was about to become the object of bloodshed.

Late on the eighteenth, Gilmor and his men crept forward in the dark of night and rushed the strong Federal picket left to secure the bridge. Initially, the attack went well, but the Federals rallied and saved the bridge. According to Gilmor's report, his men killed and wounded several of the enemy and took fifteen prisoners while losing only three wounded. Gilmor himself barely escaped death or serious injury himself. At least one of Gilmor's wounded men was taken to Mount Airy, where the ladies carefully provided medical attention.

In December, Lee sent General Jubal A. Early to the valley to take command of all Southern troops in the area. Being unable to rely on the Confederate Commissary Department, Lee intended to use Early's troops to gather supplies badly need for the coming spring campaign. He also returned Jones's cavalry brigade. Jones's brigade contained several companies of county troopers, and their homecoming for Christmas was a special delight to loved ones and family members. Winter was especially welcome for these men because it gave them a chance to get fresh mounts before spring.

8

The Hard War

As 1864 opened, Shenandoah County was free of Federal troops, but bitter feelings between Union men and local authorities continued. Many men suspected of harboring deserters were interrogated, and a number were arrested. The feelings ran so high that a number of Union supporters who had stuck it out in the county gave up and went to the comparative safety of Union lines. Many families were very weary of war but still believed the Confederacy would prevail. Shortages were now commonplace, and rampant inflation was at hand, but life continued. Shortly, spring and summer would come, and most expected that would bring victory followed by peace and independence. Little did the locals know that summer would bring with it the worst times of their lives.

Early in the war, Federals seemed content to remain on the defensive, sending only the occasional scouting patrol. Jubal Early used the lull in fighting to conduct a series of raids into West Virginia. Lee's army was extremely short on food, and the border counties held the promise of large herds of cattle. The only sizable Confederate units remaining in the valley were a single cavalry brigade in camp at Mount Jackson and a strong picket force at Fisher's Hill.

In January, the Federals launched two scouting patrols that came into the county, but both were easily repelled. The lack of Federal action resulted in Lincoln replacing Brigadier General Kelley with Major General Franz Sigel. Sigel, a German immigrant educated in European military schools, was immensely popular among the large German-American population, and his appointment was an attempt by Lincoln to win support for the war from that sector of the Northern population. Originally commissioned as a brigadier general in the fall of 1861, Sigel's stellar performance at the Battle of Pea Ridge won his promotion to major general. Unfortunately, Sigel's performance in the valley was not so stellar; in fact, Sigel would go down in history as a "walking military disaster, who bawled out orders in German when rattled."

On February 29, 1864, most of the cavalry forces stationed in the valley, including the Laurel Brigade, were called east to oppose a Federal raid toward Richmond, leaving the defense of the valley to General John D. Imboden's Northwestern Brigade. Imboden had done a masterful job of guarding Lee's wagon train filled with wounded after the defeat at Gettysburg. Now, he was being called on to block Federal forces coming into the central Shenandoah Valley from two separate directions. Not only did Imboden have to worry about the Federals, but he also had to find forage and grain for his horses. In a dispatch, Imboden stated that "Shenandoah and the country below is so completely exhausted of forage and grain that it is with great difficulty and labor, and constant controversies with the people that even a small picket force can be supplied."

Imboden also complained to Lee that General Early was making increasingly disparaging remarks about his command. Early did not care for the cavalry, so Lee was probably not surprised about Early's remarks. Lee politely appointed Major General John C. Breckinridge to command the forces in the valley and recalled Early for duty with the main army at Fredericksburg. Breckinridge had also fought in the west at Shiloh, Chickamauga and Missionary Ridge before coming east to assume command of the Department of Southwestern Virginia. He was a widely known politician, having served two terms in the U.S. House of Representatives prior to becoming the youngest vice president in the history of the United States. Breckinridge quickly transferred his headquarters to Staunton to protect vital Confederate interests located there. During the months of March and April, the opposing commanders were busy finding troops and supplies for their respective commands.

"UPON THE PROGRESS OF OUR ARMS... ALL ELSE CHIEFLY DEPENDS"

It was not only the South that was growing war weary; many Northern newspapers were also whipping up support for ending the war. The

Democratic Party made ending the war its central focus, believing this cause would bring Lincoln's defeat in the coming presidential election. Lincoln understood that despite all the Union victories, the Confederacy still existed, and a complete victory was the only way to save the Union and his reelection. Lincoln summed up the situation by saying, "Upon the progress of our arms...all else chiefly depends."

Lincoln solved his command problems once and for all with the appointment of Ulysses S. Grant as the commanding general of all Northern armies. With Grant now in command, a new level of planning and coordination took place everywhere. Central to Grant's plan for ending the war were two main campaigns: Sherman's advance from Chattanooga to Atlanta in the west and the destruction of Robert E. Lee's Army of Northern Virginia in the east. To defeat Lee, Grant knew he had to do two things: 1) severely curtail Lee's supplies and reinforcements and 2) tie Lee's forces down. Lee's successes over the last three years were based on his ability to move around the battlefield and exploit his opponent's weaknesses by overwhelming the enemy in those weak spots. To prevent supplies and reinforcements from reaching Lee from the Shenandoah Valley, Grant called for Franz Sigel to proceed up the valley and cut the rail lines from the west. Meanwhile, Benjamin Butler's Army of the James was to march along the James River and cut the railroad between Petersburg and Richmond. If these two expeditions succeeded, Lee would have to fight without significant reinforcements and with his supply lines almost entirely broken. Grant, traveling with the Army of the Potomac, would hammer Lee's army continuously, not allowing him to maneuver into a favorable position.

All three Virginia campaigns were launched in early May. On May 4, Grant and the Army of the Potomac crossed the Rapidan River, hoping to march through the Wilderness before Lee could react. Instead, Lee attacked while Grant's men were still in the tangled forests. The Battle of the Wilderness set the tone for the next month's fighting. Lee won a tactical victory, inflicting 17,000 casualties while only suffering 7,500. Lee was satisfied with his army's achievements in the Wilderness, but in the valley, more sadness came as the lists of dead and wounded were read.

Unlike previous commanders, at the end of the battle, Grant did not retreat but instead moved southeast toward Spotsylvania Court House in an attempt to get past Lee's right wing. Lee moved in time to prevent Grant from seizing the road junction at Spotsylvania. Fighting continued around Spotsylvania from May 8 to May 21. The most infamous part of this battle occurred around a mule shoe salient in the Confederate line. The fighting that followed was some of the bloodiest of the war. It went on all day and earned the tip of the mule shoe its more famous name: the "Bloody Angle of Spotsylvania." At Bloody Angle, most of the men in the Stonewall Brigade, which included many county soldiers, were killed, wounded or captured. Once again, sadness swept throughout the county as casualty lists were posted.

As the armies battered each other in Virginia, citizens back home crowded newspaper and telegraph offices in a mood of "painful suspense [that] unfits the mind for mental activity." These were "fearfully critical, anxious days," wrote a New Yorker, in which "the destiny of the continent for centuries" would be decided.

After two battles, Grant had lost over thirty thousand men, but he had inflicted eighteen thousand casualties on Lee. Despite this imbalance in losses, if Butler and Sigel could prevent Lee from being reinforced, then Grant's plan was well on its way to success. However, both were failing.

Butler's mission was a complete failure, and now it was up to Sigel in the Shenandoah. By the end of April, Sigel had amassed nearly seven thousand men. Now he was preparing to follow Grant's orders, but most of his cavalry had already been drawn off to West Virginia thanks to partisan activity by John H. McNeil and Imboden.

As Sigel began a slow advance up the valley, Breckinridge dispatched Imboden with his cavalry brigade to Mount Jackson. By May 5, Sigel's main army was at Winchester. Lethargically, his column moved up the valley, harassed by Confederate irregulars along the way. At Strasburg, Sigel divided his cavalry, sending part of it east to the Luray Valley. He continued on with his main force led by cavalry under the command of Major Charles Otis of the Twenty-first New York. Above Maurertown, Sigel's vanguard met Captain Davis's picket, which pushed the Federals back to Strasburg. Two days later, Sigel's cavalry reconnoitered in the area of Woodstock, while the Federal infantry moved to Cedar Creek, finding that a band of guerrillas had burned the bridge. After a day's delay, Sigel crossed Cedar Creek and entered Strasburg, while cavalry continuously skirmished with Sturgis's and Gilmor's picket forces now near Mount Jackson. Near Hawkinstown, Gilmor was wounded in the back and taken to Mount Airy, where he was treated by the Meem ladies.

In the afternoon, Sigel's main force entered Woodstock, where he began to prepare earthworks for an expected attack by Breckinridge. At the local telegraph office, Sigel's scouts found a pile of dispatches. From these dispatches, Sigel learned that Imboden's cavalry was his only opposition.

As Sigel moved up the valley, his line of supply, stretching all the way back to Martinsburg, became increasingly exposed to attack. Colonel John

S. Mosby took advantage of Sigel's vulnerable supply line by dispatching two companies under the command of Captain William H. Chapman to attack. Chapman's small force waited at Cedar Creek until a supply train from Winchester passed heading south on pike.

With his men disguised by their oilcloths worn as a protection from the rain, he followed in its rear until the wagons were ascending Fisher's Hill. Wagons slowed, and the guard became strung all along the road winding up the side of the hill. Several wagons crashed, blocking the bridge over Tumbling Run. Chapmen chose this time to charge the rear guard. Twelve Federals were killed and wounded, nineteen were made prisoners and twenty-three horses were secured. Chapman's command dispersed, and the men vanished into the countryside.

Earlier on May 11, Sigel had dispatched Colonel William H. Boyd with three hundred cavalrymen to scout east through the Blue Ridge Mountains to Luray. At Luray, Boyd would turn west, crossing the New Market Gap and hopefully getting between Breckinridge, whom Sigel expected to be attacking Woodstock, and his headquarters at Staunton. Of course, by this time Sigel knew the main part of Breckinridge's troops was still in the Staunton area, but Boyd did not know this. On May 13, Boyd's troopers reached New Market Gap, where they could plainly see the military camps located in the valley below. Believing, against all advice, that these were the Federal camps, Boyd ordered his force to proceed down the steep road to the bridge across Smith Creek east of the town. Unfortunately for the Federals, the camps belonged to Imboden's brigade, and they could clearly view the Federal troopers as they descended the mountain. The Eighteenth Virginia Cavalry saddled up and quickly rode to a ford above the bridge where they could cross Smith Creek and get into Boyd's rear. Imboden, a former artillerist early in the war, took personal command of McClanahan's guns. The Twenty-third Virginia Cavalry, led by Colonel Robert White, was instructed to slow the Federals' progress after they crossed the bridge. Just as the Federals cleared the bridge, White's men fired a volley into the ranks of the Federals, unhorsing some and creating confusion among the rest. Boyd's men attempted to re-form and charge White, but this attempt was hampered by the fire from McClanahan's guns. In desperation, the remaining Federals wheeled about and raced back up the road in the direction from which they had come. Some broke through the Eighteenth's line and escaped, but many did not. Some dismounted and ran in all directions to the safety of the mountains. Boyd's force was completely decimated, losing at least 125 men and close to two hundred horses.

Not only was Sigel ignorant of Boyd's debacle, but he also still had no idea where Breckinridge was. On May 13, Sigel dispatched two infantry regiments under Colonel Augustus Moor and the First New York (Lincoln) Cavalry, under Major Timothy Quinn, to seek out Breckinridge's position. As Moor was leaving Woodstock, he met the scattered bands of cavalrymen from Boyd's detachment. Moor and Quinn came into contact with some of Imboden's troops near Mount Jackson on the fourteenth, forced them across the North Fork and took possession of the bridge. Pleased with their success, Moor pushed on to New Market, nineteen miles from Sigel's position at Woodstock. Sigel learned of Moor's movement and also that Breckinridge was on the march late at night on the fourteenth. Sigel, in his battle report, claimed that he planned to take up a defensive position at Mount Jackson, so he ordered the troops to move at 5:00 a.m. on the fifteenth. They arrived at Mount Jackson at about 10:00 a.m. At Mount Jackson, Sigel claims he received information from Colonel Moor that he was in a very good position. Other reports from New Market indicated that the Federal commanders on the scene were "eager for the fight." A member of General Stahel's staff reported that Breckinridge was in force in their front and that "if I would send two batteries they would be of excellent use." For a variety of ridiculous reasons, Sigel decided to push on to New Market.

Colonel Moor was deployed into a line of battle through the village west across Manor's Hill. Originally, Moor was only facing the troops of Imboden's brigade deployed in such a fashion as to create the impression of a much stronger force. McClanahan's battery was in position on the crest of Shirley's Hill, where it dueled for nearly two hours with the Federal batteries of Captains Chatham Ewing, located west of the pike on the crest of Manor's Hill, and Alonzo Snow, located in the cemetery of the Lutheran church in town.

Early on the fourteenth, Imboden rode south to meet with General Breckinridge at Lacey's Springs. As the two generals lunched, they received news of the Federal advance beyond Rude's Hill. Breckinridge directed Imboden to withdraw his men south of New Market after dark and await the arrival of Breckinridge during the night. Once the commands had joined, Breckinridge would make final plans to receive Sigel's expected attack. Imboden rode back to New Market, where he repelled several Federal attacks by skirmishers before withdrawing his forces south of the town to the area of Shirley's Hill. It had rained hard throughout the day, and the rain continued into the evening. The coming battle would be remembered in history thanks to the valor of a cadet battalion from the

Virginia Military Institute. It would also be one of the last Confederate victories in the Shenandoah Valley.

While troops of both sides were familiar sights to New Market residents, they had never experienced the horror of war that was coming to their doorstep. In the town of New Market, the inhabitants boarded up doors and windows and generally sought refuge from the artillery barrage in the cellars of their homes. Men drove their carriages and livestock away to keep them from being taken by the opposing forces. Some even sheltered smaller animals in their homes and hid prized possessions in secret places between floors.

After midnight, Breckinridge advanced with most of his command north along the Valley Pike from near Lacey's Springs. By 6:00 a.m., he had reached the Shenandoah County line. He halted near here to reconnoiter, and about 8:00 a.m. he sent his cavalry and artillery forward to harass Moor's Union force. Confederate artillery unlimbered and fired from the heights of Shirley's Hill. Moor established his line along the old River Road with artillery deployed as it had been the day before. The rest of Sigel's infantry was spread out along the pike as far north as Edinburg. Brigadier General Julius Stahel arrived about 8:30 a.m. and ordered Moor to withdraw some of his troops to Bushong's Hill. While Breckinridge waited for the rest of

The Shirley House, located at the foot of Shirley's Hill. The building is currently used as the headquarters of the Shenandoah Battlefields Foundation.

his infantry to reach the field, Union guns in the cemetery and Confederate guns on Shirley's Hill exchanged fire.

About 11:00 a.m., Sigel finally arrived on the battlefield and established temporary headquarters at the Rice House. After reviewing Moor's dispositions, he ordered his line withdrawn to a stronger position on Bushong's Hill, stretching between a bend in the North Fork and Smith's Creek. Sigel brought up fourteen guns to support his position, leaving DuPont's battery at Rude's Hill awaiting orders. He placed cavalry on his left flank between the Valley Pike and Smith's Creek. Breckinridge deployed on both sides of the pike and advanced his infantry in force, driving back the Federal skirmishers. Imboden crossed Smith's Creek with his cavalry and attempted to outflank Sigel by moving north along the east bank. By 12:30 p.m., Sigel had withdrawn entirely from the town of New Market. The 18th Connecticut and the 123rd Ohio Infantry Regiments resisted the Southern advance on Manor's Hill before joining the main battle line at Bushong's.

About 2:00 p.m., Breckinridge launched an all-out assault against the Union position on Bushong's Hill, using the Twenty-sixth, Thirtieth, Fifty-first and Sixty-second Virginia Mounted Infantry. The Sixty-second,

The Bushong home on the New Market Battlefield.

although normally a mounted unit, fought on foot this day and suffered more than 50 percent casualties. When the Confederate attack stalled under heavy small-arms and artillery fire, the VMI battalion was ordered to fill the gap in the line near the Bushong House.

About 2:30 p.m., General Stahel's Union cavalry attacked straight up the Valley Pike, riding directly into massed artillery, which Breckinridge had shifted east from Shirley's Hill. Stahel was repulsed with heavy casualties. Soon after the failure of the cavalry charge, Sigel directed a confused infantry attack, which was soon repulsed.

Confederate sharpshooters from Woodson's Missouri boys and the Sixty-second Mounted Infantry began picking off Union gunners on Bushong's Hill north of the Bushong farm, so Sigel ordered the batteries withdrawn. Limbers were brought forward, but hitching up the guns did not go smoothly. When the artillery fire slackened, Breckinridge ordered a general advance and swept the Union line off Bushong's Hill. In this assault, the VMI cadets captured a gun and many men of the Thirty-fourth Massachusetts.

The monument to the Fifty-fourth Pennsylvania Infantry Regiment along the Valley Pike on the New Market Battlefield.

To the east near the Valley Pike, elements of the Thirty-fourth Massachusetts and Fifty-fourth Pennsylvania Infantry continued to resist, covering the Union retreat. The men of the Fifty-fourth Pennsylvania scattered in the cedars near the pike kept the oncoming Confederates busy and allowed many of the men from other units and the supply wagons that had been brought forward to escape.

The Confederates regrouped and came on again, applying more pressure. The Fifty-fourth Pennsylvania and the Thirty-fourth Massachusetts were eventually driven back, and the Federal forces were now in the midst of a rout.

On his own initiative, Captain Henry DuPont brought up his battery to cover the retreat. He unlimbered first near the Harshburger House and then withdrew his pieces rearward en echelon as the Confederates advanced. Sigel fell back to his supports at the Cedar Grove Dunker Church and cemetery and organized a holding action, while his confused troops reorganized. DuPont's artillery continued to slow the pursuit.

The front door of the Henkel home in New Market. Damage to the door came from a Federal bayonet used to gain entrance to the house during the Battle of New Market.

The scene in New Market after the battle was a grim one. Windows had been shattered by the artillery, and dead horses lay strewn about.

Wounded soldiers covered in mud were being carried in from the fields. Sigel lost 96 dead, 520 wounded and 225 captured or missing. Breckinridge's losses were fewer but still significant, with 43 dead and 474 wounded and missing. The Confederate surgeons, together with the local doctors, spent a long night caring for the wounded. Almost every suitable structure became a hospital, including many homes and barns.

The next day, burial details were sent to recover

the dead. The Federals sent an ambulance filled with medical supplies under a flag of truce to New Market but refused to send soldiers to bury the Federal dead. Breckinridge had the Confederate dead interred in St. Matthew's Church, but the townspeople refused to allow the dead Federals to be buried there. A plot was found along the pike north of the village between St. Matthew's Church and the Rice home, and the Federal dead were quickly and carelessly buried in shallow graves. The corps of cadets gathered that morning for a special ceremony to bury five of their own. The ceremony took place in the cemetery behind the St. Mathews Church. Sometime later, the cadets were disinterred and moved to VMI, where they were reburied.

The following day, May 17, Breckinridge marched his command toward Staunton, leaving Imboden once again as the ranking Confederate commander in the lower valley. At Staunton, Breckinridge loaded his men in the cars of the Virginia Central Railroad and journeyed east to aid Lee in the defense of the Confederate capital.

Sigel withdrew to the north banks of Cedar Creek, where he went into camp. Sigel placed Colonel George D. Wells with two companies of infantry in a secure position south of Strasburg. On May 20, Colonel Wells sent scouts into Little Fort Valley, where they ascended Three-Top Mountain and found the Confederate signal station to be abandoned.

Hunter's Raid

Sigel's failure meant the end of his command, and the end came swiftly. Late in the evening on May 21, Major General David Hunter suddenly arrived at the Belle Grove mansion at Cedar Creek, and he immediately assumed command of the Department of West Virginia. Hunter was a Virginian who had a number of relatives living in the Shenandoah Valley.

Unlike many of his West Point contemporaries from Virginia, Hunter did not side with the North because of his unquenchable hatred of slavery. Hunter's reputation as a resentful, quick-tempered and insensitive commander was well earned. Early in the war, while serving as a department commander, Hunter had recruited the first Negro regiment ever in the United States Army. Because of that action, he got his nickname: "Black Dave." Lincoln immediately rescinded Hunter's orders and disbanded the black regiment. Hunter was then transferred to a command farther west.

Belle Grove mansion, the headquarters for Federal generals Sigel, Hunter and Sheridan. General Ramseur's body was taken here following the Battle of Cedar Creek.

By 1864, Hunter's reputation was restored, and the administration was in agreement with Hunter's former actions.

Hunter's specific orders for the coming campaign were to march south to capture Staunton, Lexington and Lynchburg if possible. Along the way, the troops were instructed to "live off the land" and to destroy the Virginia Central Railroad so thoroughly that it would take four weeks to rebuild.

Hunter quickly improved the security of his command. Colonel Wells's picket forces were heavily reinforced. Infantry companies were sent to Hupp's Hill. Wells asked whether he should occupy the signal station on Three-Top Mountain and was directed not to do so until he received orders. That same night, a Confederate signal party occupied the mountain and was observed signaling with rockets to other posts up the valley. One of Wells's picket forces, a small cavalry force under the command of Captain Michael Auer, Company A, Fifteenth New York Cavalry, was surprised by Imboden's scouts and, after a sharp skirmish, had eleven Federal troopers captured. Hunter's wrath was immediate and was entirely in keeping with his reputation. Captain Auer and his superior, Major Henry Russell, were both removed from command and

The Painter home, located near Pugh's Run.

dishonorably discharged from United States service in a lengthy order dated May 24, 1864.

The Federal army broke camp at 10:30 a.m. on May 26, moving through Strasburg to Pugh's Run just north of Woodstock. As the Federals marched from Strasburg, Hunter had a large barn burned on suspicion that its owners had harbored bushwhackers. At Pugh's Run, Hunter's men dug rifle pits and took up defensive positions. Hunter's headquarters were established at the Painter home on Pugh's Run.

Hunter remained in position there for several days, awaiting the arrival of a large shipment of shoes for his men. Hunter dispatched troops into the countryside to confiscate food for his men and forage for his horses. This was not the first time enemy troops had seized what they needed, but this time there was much less to take. The Confederate tax-in-kind, which required farmers to give the government 10 percent of all agricultural products and livestock raised for slaughter, put a tremendous burden on valley farmers. Confederate commissary officers, who always paid only a fraction of what crops were worth, were constantly harassing farmers to sell more of their decreasing surpluses. The hardening attitudes of many of Hunter's men did little to help. Many of those foraging the countryside for Hunter had been present at New Market, and the embarrassing sting of that defeat was fresh in their minds. General Julius Stahel was reprimanded by Hunter for the pillaging being committed by his troopers. Hunter accused the troops of straggling into houses and "carrying off dresses, ornaments, books, money and doing wanton injury to furniture." He also accused Stahel's men of leaving camp in squads without authorization and committing a variety of other depredations. Hunter was an arsonist but apparently not a thief.

As Hunter marched south, Imboden's scouts watched them from the Massanutten and sent signals to Imboden regarding Hunter's progress. Imboden forwarded the information about the Federal advance directly to Robert E. Lee. Lee replied that he had no reinforcements to send at that time. Lee suggested that Imboden mobilize the Home Guard and contact General "Grumble" Jones at Abingdon, Virginia, about the possibility of reinforcements. Imboden followed these suggestions and began to assemble a makeshift resistance force for an expected confrontation south of Harrisonburg.

On May 29, Hunter's army was again placed in motion and marched south at daylight. While at Woodstock, Hunter decided to burn the Hollingsworth Hotel as an example to the population but was dissuaded by the articulate argument of his cousin and chief of staff David Strother. At Edinburg, Hunter ordered that a large quantity of salt be destroyed. By this time, salt was as precious as gold. He continued his advance through Mount Jackson, where he stopped to visit the Federals still in the hospital and leave them with supplies. He then moved to Rude's Hill, where his headquarters were established at the home of Reverend A.R. Rude. Early the next morning, the march was continued to New Market. Here, the Federals paused to reinter the remains of their hastily buried comrades killed two weeks earlier. Imboden's scouts managed the capture of a small Federal picket east of New Market.

General Jones agreed to join Imboden with about three thousand men in the vicinity of Staunton in hopes of defending that important town. The combined Southern forces established a makeshift line of defense in the village of Piedmont on June 5. Hunter attacked and, after some very bitter fighting, defeated the Confederates, killing or capturing about 1,500 men. General Jones was killed during the height of the fighting.

Hunter's troops took Staunton and managed to destroy much of the Confederate logistical operation there; they also damaged but did not destroy the railroad there. Hunter then continued on to Lexington, where he burned Governor Letcher's home and the Virginia Military Institute. From there, he continued on toward Lynchburg.

Robert E. Lee was concerned about Hunter's advances in the valley, which threatened critical railroad lines and provisions for his forces. He sent Jubal

Early's men to Lynchburg to sweep Union forces from the valley and, if possible, to menace Washington, D.C., hoping to compel Grant to dilute his forces around Petersburg. Here was Lee's last chance to seize the initiative once again and force a superior enemy into doing his bidding, as he had done in 1862. The problem was that it was 1864, not 1862, and Early was no Jackson.

Early's troops arrived in time to stop Hunter west of Lynchburg. Hunter began to withdraw, but instead of moving back down the valley, he elected to retreat into West Virginia, leaving the valley wide open for Early. After following Hunter briefly, Early returned to the Valley Pike and quickly moved down the whole length of the valley without opposition. He bypassed Harpers Ferry, crossed the Potomac River and advanced into Maryland. Upon learning that Early was in Maryland, Grant dispatched Major General Horatio G. Wright with a large force, including the Sixth Corps and part of the Nineteenth Corps, to reinforce Washington and drive Early back into Virginia.

After brushing aside a small force at Monocacy, Early approached the outer defenses of Washington on July 11. He probed the defenses of Fort Stevens, but when Wright's reinforcement arrived, Early decided against a general attack. He began to withdraw back toward the valley with Wright's troops in pursuit. General Early briefly stopped the Federals at Castleman's Ferry on the western bank of the Shenandoah River and then continued on to Winchester, where his men could rest from their long, tortuous march in the oppressive summer heat. After a brief stay, Early moved to a more secure position at Strasburg on July 19. The movement required the evacuation of the military hospitals and storage depots around Winchester. To cover the evacuation, Early left Major General Stephen Dodson Ramseur's division at Winchester with orders to stay within the city's defensive works and not to precipitate any unnecessary engagements with the enemy. On July 20, Brigadier General W.W. Averell's division attacked Ramseur in what became a Southern debacle. Averell captured four pieces of Confederate artillery and nearly three hundred prisoners. With this defeat, Early withdrew his army to a stronger defensive position at Fisher's Hill. General Wright concluded that the Confederates were merely fighting a rear-guard action and that Early was leaving the valley. With the threat to Washington seemingly over, Wright withdrew the Sixth Corps and the Nineteenth Corps from the valley to return to Petersburg, leaving only the three divisions of the Army of the Kanawha under George Crook in the valley. As soon as Early learned that Wright was gone, he decided he had to attack and defeat Crook's troops in order to draw Wright's troops back to the valley. Early moved north and attacked Crook near Kernstown, defeating him handily and driving him into West Virginia and Maryland. Early followed up his success by sending his cavalry across the Potomac and into Pennsylvania, where it burned the city of Chambersburg in retaliation for Hunter's previous destruction in the valley. Grant quickly reacted by returning the Sixth Corps and the Nineteenth Corps to the valley.

THE VALLEY CAMPAIGN OF 1864

Grant knew that the Shenandoah Valley was a special place to the Confederates. To many Virginians, the valley seemed to have an almost mystical quality about it. The Confederate army had used the valley both to feed its men and to launch embarrassing attacks into the North. The Federal army had suffered repeated failures there for three years. Early's threat to Washington, Crook's defeat at Second Kernstown and the burning of Chambersburg forced Grant to move decisively to end Confederate dominance in the Shenandoah Valley. In addition to the Sixth Corps and the XIX Corps, Grant added two fully equipped divisions of cavalry. More importantly, Grant consolidated the various military districts of the region under a single commander. The commander he selected was Major General Philip H. Sheridan, who had served with Grant in the west. Sheridan assumed command of the new Middle Military District at Harpers Ferry on August 7, 1864.

Grant gave Sheridan two missions. First, he was to "put himself south of the enemy" and destroy Early's army, preferably by outmaneuvering him. Grant had no interest in another slugfest with its bloody consequences, as had been taking place in the campaign for Richmond. Second, Sheridan was to take or destroy anything that might be of use to the enemy, especially the food that was supplying the Confederate armies. This was harsh warfare, but Grant's aim was to win the war as quickly as possible. Grant believed that more lives would be lost if the war were prolonged than if the valley itself became a military target. While Sheridan's devastation of the valley was to cause much hardship, his aim was to destroy the surplus crops that could feed an army, not to cause starvation among the population.

To accomplish his mission, Sheridan had an army of 34,000 infantry, 6,400 cavalry and numerous batteries of artillery. As had happened so often in the past, Union intelligence overestimated the size of Early's army. With reinforcements soon to be sent from Lee, Early had about 23,000 men, although Federal intelligence placed his strength at 40,000. With this seeming disadvantage in troop strength and Grant's instructions to avoid a bloodbath, Sheridan prepared carefully for his coming campaign. Lee reinforced Early by sending Major General Joseph Kershaw's infantry division, Fitzhugh Lee's cavalry division and Cutshaw's artillery battalion, all under the overall command of Lieutenant General Richard Anderson.

On August 11, Sheridan advanced on Winchester, so Early withdrew to Cedar Creek and, the following day, to Fisher's Hill, where he began building earthworks. General Early kept a strong picket in Strasburg in order to control the town. Sheridan established his camp at Cedar Creek and sent out pickets to Hupp's Hill. Sheridan pushed on into Strasburg, and a number of skirmishes took place on August 14.

Seeing the tactical importance of the Confederate signal station on Three-Top Mountain, Sheridan sent a sortie up the mountain to seize the position. The Confederate signalmen were not prepared for an attack, so they abandoned the position. Realizing the tactical value of the location, Early sent Captain Benjamin J. Keller and one hundred of his best sharpshooters from the Sixtieth Georgia Regiment to regain the position. It was mid-August, so the weather was exceedingly hot when the contending forces faced off against each other near Sand Spring on the Fort Valley side of the mountain. Both sides lost at least one man killed and three wounded, but the Georgians succeeded in retaking the position. Sheridan had been ordered to move cautiously and avoid a defeat, particularly if Early were reinforced by Lee. With these instructions in mind, Sheridan withdrew through Newtown and Berryville to Halltown. Along the way, Sheridan's men set fire to several barns and mills.

Both Early and Sheridan probed each other's positions using brigade-sized patrols to gather information. Numerous deadly skirmishes took place, with losses to both sides, but Sheridan chose not to bring on a general attack. In judging Sheridan's performance thus far, General Early considered him a "timid" commander. With the Potomac protecting his flank, Sheridan strengthened his frontal position and extended his lines while he waited for his chance. Sheridan's lack of progress worried Lincoln, and eventually even Grant, who made two visits to the valley to prod Sheridan into action.

On September 15, Anderson, along with Kershaw's division and Cutshaw's artillery battalion, was recalled to Petersburg. Despite his reduced force, Early tried to create the appearance of a much stronger force by spreading out his remaining divisions over a distance of more than thirty miles from Winchester to Martinsburg. As soon as Sheridan learned from a unionist spy that Anderson had left the valley, he decided to attack immediately while the Confederate army was scattered. Sheridan planned to attack Winchester from the east, cutting off Early from the rest of the valley. Sheridan concentrated his force at Berryville and readied his attack.

Well before daylight on September 19, Sheridan began a march through the Berryville Gorge just east of Winchester. The wagon train of the Sixth Corps got tangled up with the troops of from the Nineteenth Corps and almost halted the assault before it began. With "much energy and profanity," Sheridan straightened out the jam, got his troops into line and began the attack. The battle lasted most of the day, with Sheridan eventually forcing the outnumbered Confederates into a small area. Northern cavalry, with their rapid-firing carbines, now played a conspicuous role. Two divisions of horsemen thundered down on Early's left in an old-fashioned saber charge. The Confederate line fell apart and began to run from the field. This is when the bulk of the two thousand Confederate prisoners was captured. "We have just sent them whirling through Winchester," wired Sheridan's chief of staff in a phrase that looked good in the newspapers, "and we are after them to-morrow."

Dr. Hunter H. McGuire was able to remove all but the most severely wounded from the hospitals and homes of Winchester before the Federals swept into town. Most of the wounded were loaded into crowded ambulances to begin a miserable journey south to Woodstock, where their first rest, examination and care were provided. Private John Worsham of the Twenty-first Virginia Infantry was wounded in the knee late in the action. Reaching Winchester, he was hastily loaded into an ambulance that was wildly driven through the night. After a short rest the following morning, he stated:

> I prevailed on the driver…to pull off my boot—it was full of blood and running over the top! Soon after it was pulled off, my wound seemed to stop bleeding, and I proceeded more comfortably. We rode until four o'clock in the afternoon, when we halted at a church in Woodstock. Here the ladies brought to the wounded fruit, flowers, eatables, water and bandages, and made themselves very useful to two or three hundred wounded. A surgeon cut open my pants and drawers, and examined my wound and dressed it—this was the first time it was seen even by myself…About sunset the wounded were put into wagons on a little straw and started up the pike.

Worsham finally had the ball removed from his leg after reaching Charlottesville some three days later. Early's losses included General Robert E. Rodes, killed instantly by a shell fragment, and General Zebulon York, a brigade commander in Gordon's Division, whose arm was shattered so badly that it required amputation. Major General Fitzhugh Lee received a painful wound requiring him to pass command of the cavalry to Major General Lunsford L. Lomax. Colonel George S. Patton, grandfather of the famous World War II hero, was mortally wounded and left at Winchester, where he later died. Early transferred General Stephen D. Ramseur to the command of Rodes's division and elevated Brigadier General John Pegram to command Ramseur's division.

Early moved into his former positions on Fisher's Hill, hoping to gain some time to reorganize, but Sheridan, sensing final victory in the Shenandoah, moved forward as rapidly as possible. At the close of the day on September 20, Sheridan's camps stretched from Hupp's Hill back to Cedar Creek. As darkness fell, Sheridan's advance pushed on into the northern part of Strasburg. Sheridan established his headquarters

A sketch of Confederate officers observing Federal troops. *From James E. Taylor's* Sketchbook.

on the Stickleys' farm. The following morning, the Federals pushed the Confederates out of Strasburg and into the hills south of town. Sheridan and his senior commanders displayed some concern over Early's naturally strong position on Fisher's Hill.

From his signal station at the northern end of Massanutten Mountain, Early's signalmen watched the Federals move about and signaled that information to Early. Early augmented his reconnaissance by establishing another signal station on Round Hill.

Sheridan was right to be concerned about the natural strength of Early's position. Fisher's Hill is actually a series of natural ridges that rise across the valley from east to west in a line stretching over four miles. The eastern end of the position is quite steep, heavily wooded and sharply drops down to the Shenandoah River, which runs north along the base of Massanutten. Tumbling Run, a brook very appropriately named, flows east from the Back Road along almost the entire length of the base on Fisher's Hill until it finally empties into the North Fork. The stream's steep banks were not easily fordable, except where the area's farmers had built crossings.

The Confederate positions were strongest at the center and on the right flank. Wharton's division, on the Confederate right flank, entrenched along the high bluff overlooking Miller's Bottoms, extended to the left to cover the Valley Pike as it was aligned at this time. The modern route of the Valley Pike cuts through part of Wharton's position. Gordon's division deployed from the Valley Pike across the roadbed of the Manassas Gap Railroad to near the Middle Road above the village of Fisher's Hill. Pegram's division, which had formerly belonged to Ramseur, was positioned on Gordon's left, and Ramseur's division extended the line west to a high hill that became known after the war as "Ramseur's Hill." The weakest part of the Confederate line was to Ramseur's left. This part of the line was assigned to an inadequately armed cavalry division commanded by General Lomax. The line held by Lomax extended northwest beyond the Back Road. Without enough troops to man it, Lomax's position was held with little more than a skirmish line.

To mask his deployments, Early put forward a strong skirmish line on Quarry Hill, Flint Hill and School House Ridge north of Tumbling Run. Early's artillery commanded all approaches along the pike, the railroad and the Middle Road, but the advanced Confederate skirmish positions north of Tumbling Run were not supported by artillery. A brigade of Confederate cavalry and a battery of horse artillery were placed on Sandy Hook east of the North Fork.

"Ramseur's Hill" on the Fisher's Hill battlefield. It was here that General Ramseur's Confederate division attempted to prevent Sheridan's army from turning the Confederate flank.

About noon on the twenty-first, Sheridan advanced his army south and west from Strasburg, massing the bulk of the Sixth Corps in a horseshoe formation on the plateau north of Flint Hill. The XIX Corps, badly battered at Winchester, was placed on the left, to the east of the railroad. Its skirmish line extended back through Strasburg to cover the fords over the North Fork and the road to Front Royal. Both corps began to dig entrenchments. Crook's VIII Corps was held in reserve in the woods near Strasburg and out of sight of the Confederates on Signal Knob. Averell's cavalry division covered the Back Road. The rest of Sheridan's cavalry was sent via Front Royal to advance up the Luray Valley. Sheridan moved his headquarters to the George Hupp House.

While the Federals built their trenches, skirmishing increased as troops moved into position and felt out their opposition. Unable to actually view the main Confederate line because of the intervening knolls called Flint Hill, Sheridan ordered Wright to seize the position. The Flint Hill knolls were defended by a reinforced skirmish line barricaded behind U-shaped structures made of fence rails called "hog pens." It took several attempts, the last one with overwhelming manpower, to dislodge the Confederates from their hog pens, but Flint Hill was now in Federal possession. General Wright described this movement as "of the greatest importance to the operations of the next day, as it gave us a view of the enemy's line and afforded excellent positions for artillery, of which we availed ourselves in the more important struggle of the 22nd." The Federals threw up rifle pits and bivouacked on the hills within rifle-musket range of the main Confederate line south of Tumbling Run.

During the night, Sheridan extended his line westward, with James B. Ricketts's division on the far right, George W. Getty's men next and Frank Wheaton connecting with the Nineteenth Corps at the railroad. After sunrise, Crook's corps was brought forward, following ravines and staying in timber to be out of sight of the Confederate signal stations. Shortly before noon, Ricketts's division seized the heights overlooking the northern tributary of Tumbling Run, while Averell's cavalry moved up the Back Road to establish a connection with Ricketts's right flank. A Federal brigade overran the pickets at School House Ridge. Federal skirmishers were now within range of the main Confederate works and began laying down a steady fire. Ricketts formed his division behind the crest of the hills and awaited Crook's attack. In the meantime, troops from Emory's Nineteenth Corps rushed Quarry Hill on the left, seizing the rebel rifle pits there. His men immediately reversed the entrenchments, giving the Union army an unbroken line of rifle pits confronting the main Confederate line on Fisher's Hill. Firing on both sides increased as the Federals brought up additional artillery batteries, and an artillery duel erupted in the vicinity of the village of Fisher's Hill. Skirmishing continued until about 4:00 p.m.

During the morning, General Crook moved two divisions to the base of Little North Mountain beyond St. Stephens Church, still unseen by the Confederate signal station on Massanutten Mountain. About 2:00 p.m., Crook began a flanking movement along the shoulder of the mountain. Crook formed his corps in two parallel columns and marched south until more than half of the command was beyond the Confederate left flank, held by Lomax's cavalry. Crook encountered only scattered fire from a few surprised pickets.

Actually, the Confederates on Signal Knob had seen some of the Federals moving along Little North Mountain and had notified Early of that fact, but apparently little or no action came from that information. About 4:00 p.m. Crook ordered his columns to face left and to charge. The soldiers charged down the side of the mountain, shouting and shooting. Lomax's men took to their horses and scattered. In their rush down the hill, Crook's divisions lost its formation, and a mass of men funneled through the ravine of the Middle Fork of Tumbling Run past the Barbe House and closed on the flank the Confederate infantry on Ramseur's Hill. A second mass funneled to the right along an old road that penetrated to the rear of the Confederate positions. Grimes's brigade of North Carolinians held out against Crook's onslaught until Ricketts ordered his division forward. The North Carolinians were now facing the enemy on two sides. With firing in their rear, Confederates troops along the rest of the line began abandoning their positions, knowing they were flanked. Sheridan now advanced his other divisions, which crossed Tumbling Run and pushed forward using the ravines. Early's army was soon in full flight, abandoning equipment and fourteen artillery pieces that could not be extricated from the works.

Early's army was in a complete state of disorganization. Troops from different units were intermingled as they fled to the rear. Several commanders began to organize fleeing troops from the left of the line at the base of Round Hill. Meanwhile, Generals Gordon, Ramseur and Pegram and staff officers including Colonel Alexander "Sandie" Pendleton established a rear guard of artillery and infantry at Prospect Hill and held off the disorganized Union pursuit. During this action, Pendleton, Stonewall Jackson's favorite staff officer, was mortally wounded, dying the following day in Woodstock. The Confederate army retreated to Narrow Passage, and the wagon train went on to Mount Jackson. Darkness and confusion among the Union victors prevented effective pursuit.

While the fighting at Fisher's Hill was in progress, Colonel Thomas T. Munford's cavalry stopped the Federal cavalry division sent by Sheridan to get in Early's rear. Sheridan remarked that if his cavalry had been successful, he could have captured Early's army.

For the second time in four days, Early was forced to retreat in disorder, and his losses were heavier than Sheridan's: 30 dead, 210 wounded and 995 missing, as compared to Sheridan's 52 dead, 457 wounded and 19 missing. The remnants of Early's army managed to escape south once more, but the Confederate force had been so badly mauled that Grant began to debate how to best move these Federal troops east to Petersburg. Sheridan had followed Grant's orders and defeated Early by maneuvering instead of with great bloodshed. General Early placed his small army in line of battle astride the pike near the Mount Jackson hospital north of the town. Early reported his defeat in a telegram dispatched to Lee from Mount Jackson at

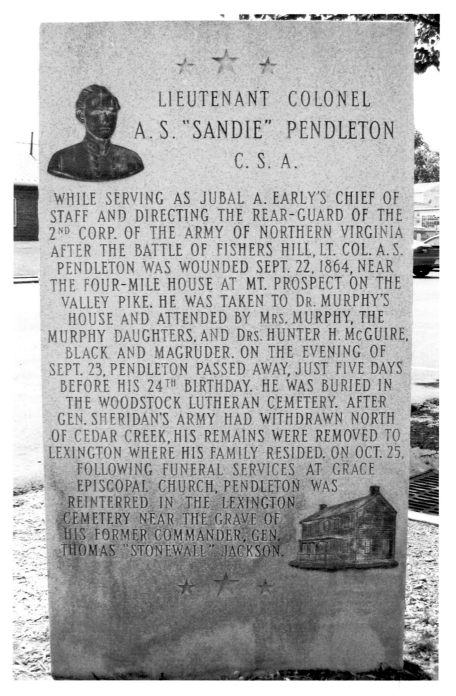

The monument to Lieutenant Colonel A.S. "Sandie" Pendleton commemorating the location where he died in Woodstock, Virginia.

4:00 a.m. Early removed medical supplies from the hospital and moved off to Rude's Hill when the Federal cavalry arrived. As the Federals entered Mount Jackson, they noted that the hospital was filled with Confederate wounded. The single building of the hospital complex that was not occupied "was most maliciously set on fire by some stragglers...and entirely destroyed."

Early continued on up the Valley Pike until he arrived in Harrisonburg, where he turned southeast, finally taking up defensive positions at Brown's Gap in the Blue Ridge. With Early out of the way, Sheridan moved into Rockingham County, where he established his headquarters at Harrisonburg. Sheridan was now in a position to carry out Grant's orders:

> *Do all the damage to railroads and crops you can. Carry off stock of all descriptions...so as to prevent further planting. If the war is to last another year, we want the Shenandoah Valley to remain a barren waste.*
>
> General Ulysses S. Grant

Sheridan dispatched his troops to all parts of Rockingham County and south into Augusta County, where the troops engaged in the systematic destruction of almost anything that might be useful to the Confederate war effort. Neither secessionists nor Union sympathizers were immune to the torch. Although the large Dunker population in Rockingham had not supported the Confederate war effort, they were forced to supply food to the Confederate government, so their farms suffered the same destruction as those of their neighbors.

On the evening of October 3, Lieutenant John R. Meigs, Sheridan's engineer officer and a personal friend, was killed by Confederate scouts near Dayton. Sheridan, believing that Meigs had been killed by civilian bushwhackers, ordered Custer, who had succeeded to the command of Wilson's cavalry division, to burn all houses within an area of five miles of the spot where Meigs was killed. The next morning, Custer began to execute his orders, but when only a few houses had been burned, the order was suspended, and Custer was ordered instead to bring in all able-bodied men as prisoners.

That same day, Custer ordered Davy Getz to be executed by gunfire. Getz was a thirty-nine-year-old mentally retarded man who had been found earlier hunting squirrels with a small rifle near Woodstock. Suspected of being a bushwhacker, he was marched to Harrisonburg behind a wagon with a rope around his neck as an example. Townspeople from Woodstock followed behind the wagon, pleading with Custer to spare his life. Realizing that their pleas were in vain, they told Custer, "You will have to sleep in a bloody grave for this."

The destruction of farms and mills in Rockingham County lasted for two more days as Sheridan began to plan for his withdrawal. Sheridan offered wagons with teams to families wishing to leave the Upper Valley with his army. Some of those families would regret their decision to go with Sheridan several days later along the Back Road in Shenandoah County. Sheridan did not fear an attack from Early, but the Rebel cavalry was growing more aggressive and was bold enough to attack a strong Federal force at Bridgewater.

At City Point, Grant was now convinced that the valley campaign was over, and he began to plan how to move Sheridan's men to Petersburg. Grant preferred Sheridan move along an overland route through Virginia, while Sheridan favored returning north and moving to Petersburg by ship down the Potomac and then up the James.

Bands of Confederate detached cavalrymen and partisan rangers were constantly roaming through the valley from Winchester to Sheridan's camps in Rockingham County, intent on disrupting Sheridan's lines of supply and communications. To protect his lines, Sheridan had earlier placed strong guard detachments at strategic points, particularly at the bridges along the Valley Pike. Every wagon train traveling in either direction was heavily guarded to prevent a surprise attack. Federal cavalry squadrons patrolled the area in search of Confederates, who, when taken into custody, were sent without delay to prisons in the North. Many of these Confederate soldiers were imprisoned under orders stating that they were "guerrillas, and not to be exchanged during the war." Research shows that the records of a number of Shenandoah County men imprisoned during this time contained this label.

Arguably, the best of the partisan rangers was Captain John H. "Hanse" McNeill and his unit, known as McNeill's Rangers. Hanse McNeill and approximately fifty rangers traveled from Hardy County on September 30 and camped at Orkney Springs. McNeill dispatched scouts to search for vulnerable targets of opportunity that his men might successfully attack. McNeill, with the rest of his command, then moved to the area just north of Edinburg. McNeill sent four of his rangers into Edinburg with orders to burn the bridge spanning Stony Creek. For whatever reason, this bridge had no Federal guards, but the citizens were afraid Sheridan would destroy the whole town if the bridge was burned.

The citizens made a desperate plea for the bridge to be spared, and the rangers relented. To escape the wrath of McNeill, the rangers came up with a novel plan to placate their commander. To create the illusion that the bridge was burning without actually setting fire to the basic structure, the partisans and the townspeople gathered armloads of moist straw, which they lit at strategic locations along the span. Smoke was pouring from the bridge by the time the four rangers rode to the outskirts of town, where Captain McNeill was observing their progress. The amount of smoke coming from the bridge convinced Hanse that his orders had been faithfully executed. The partisans had barely disappeared when the citizens of Edinburg rushed out and threw the smoldering straw into the creek. A slightly charred but structurally intact bridge still stood at Edinburg when the Federals returned.

On the afternoon of October 2, Hanse McNeill learned from John and Joseph I. Triplett, two brothers from Mount Jackson, that close to one hundred troopers from the Eighth Ohio Cavalry were camped on the bank of the North Fork guarding the bridge over the Valley Pike just south of Mount Jackson. McNeill waited for daybreak and pounced on the unwary Federals. Captain McNeill rode headlong into the Federal camp followed by his men. Some of the Federal soldiers rushed from their tents to their stacked guns, while others simply fled. Many of the Federals began to surrender, but at some point Captain McNeill fell from his horse, badly wounded by a shot in the spine. McNeill's son, Lieutenant Jesse McNeill, rushed to his father's aid. In the meantime, the task at hand was completed. Sixty Federal prisoners were captured and many others killed.

One version of McNeill's mortal wounding was that he was shot in the back by one of his own men, George Valentine. Valentine had recently been chastised by his commander for stealing chickens. Valentine was later identified as a "Jessie Scout" after shooting McNeill. The question remains: was Valentine a scout at the time of the shooting, infiltrated to kill McNeil, or did he become a Jessie Scout after killing his commander?

At any rate, McNeill was placed on his horse and taken to the home of the Reverend Addison Weller. This is the same house formerly occupied by Reverend A.R. Rude. Reverend Weller's wife treated McNeill as best she could, but it was apparent that the wound was fatal. The fear of falling into Yankee hands troubled McNeill, so his hair and beard were shaved off in the hope of concealing his identity. McNeill was now only semiconscious. The word had spread quickly that Captain McNeill had been badly wounded and that the Yankees were searching for him. Twice, scouting parties came to the Weller home in search of their ever-vanishing enemy. Both times, they failed to recognize the clean-shaven man in the dimly lighted upstairs bedroom of Mrs. Weller. In the company of several other rangers, Mrs. McNeill came to be with her husband.

On October 7, the Wellers received another houseguest when none other than Sheridan himself spent the night there. Sheridan supposedly talked to McNeill, unaware of who he was. The next day, Federal officers came to the Weller home believing that the wounded man in their care was probably McNeill. They asked the wounded man if he was not McNeill, and looking straight in their faces, he said, "I am." Hanse McNeill, one of the most feared guerrillas in the Confederacy, was now in Federal hands—at least temporarily. McNeill was too weak to be moved by horseback, so the Federals said they would send a guard and ambulance for him in several days.

That night, a small group of Confederate soldiers made their way into the area, placed Captain McNeill in a carriage supplied by General Early and moved him to Hill's Hotel in Harrisonburg, McNeill died there on November 10, 1864.

THE BURNING

Earlier, General Lee had ordered that reinforcements be sent to Early, which included the Laurel Brigade, commanded by General Rosser. Rosser, after a long, arduous ride all the way from Petersburg, arrived at Early's headquarters just days before Sheridan began to withdraw from Rockingham. General Early gave command of Fitzhugh Lee's cavalry division to Rosser and ordered him to move to Bridgewater. Early on the morning of October 6, Sheridan started the move north to carry the torch into Shenandoah County.

Sheridan's main army moved along the Valley Pike while his cavalry divisions took the side roads. Custer and the third division used the Back Road. From Bridgewater, Rosser followed Custer's trail. Fatigue turned to rage as the Laurel Brigade troopers, many of whom were from the area, moved north. Along both sides of the road, they saw farm after farm and mill after mill burned to the ground. The smoke from burning buildings darkened the sky. Dead livestock littered the fields. Near Brock's Gap, the Laurels ran into four Federals burning a barn. The infuriated Rebels shot the bluecoats without a moment of remorse and moved on.

At Brock's Gap, Rosser ran into the Federal rear guard, and a spirited skirmish ensued. Custer posted his artillery on a high hill and kept Rosser at bay until dark. Early in the morning, the Federals resumed their work. Cavalrymen assigned to the burning detail descended on the hamlet of Moore's Store on Holman's Creek. There, they destroyed everything on Joseph Moore's farm, perhaps because he was a slaveholder and well-to-do Southerner. Every building, including the mill and the house, was put to the torch without giving the family time to rescue any possessions. That night, Moore, his wife Virginia and their five children had to seek shelter elsewhere. A little farther down Holman's Creek, at Harpinetown, named after the family who lived there, the Federals burned the gristmill, along with the sawmill and several

A sketch of Federal forces setting fire to a barn during "The Burning" in October 1864. *Author's collection.*

family homes. Another half mile farther downstream was Peter Myers's mill and barn, which were also burned.

The Second Brigade, under the command of Colonel Wells, acted as guards for the long wagon train that accompanied Custer. Wells was in a difficult position, with his men being hit somewhere along their line almost constantly by small but fierce attacks. At Forestville, Wells split the long wagon train into two parts, transferring many of the wagons to the Middle Road. It was about this time that Rosser's men attacked in force. According a Pennsylvania trooper, "Rebs pitched into our rear… and captured a part of our cattle and Sheep and 8 Forges we had a sharp fight and lost about 25 men." Wells suffered the humiliation of losing most of the herd, a number of portable forges, several wagons, a few ambulances and at least twenty-five men. The capture of the forges

The scene of Custer's position north of Mill Creek when he was attacked by Rosser's Confederates on October 7, 1864.

infuriated Custer since "they were impossible to come by this far from a secure supply line."

While Wells and his men were stubbornly attempting to hold off the Confederates, the burning parties with their torches were moving along at a brisk pace; they knew very well what they could expect at the hands of the valley soldiers, whose property they were destroying.

About three o'clock in the afternoon, Rosser's pursuing column overtook the enemy at Mill Creek, with the Laurels under Colonel Dulany in the lead. On the opposite bank, the First Vermont Cavalry was strongly posted above the fords. Colonel Dulany was ordered to take a part of the Seventh and White's Battalions and cross at a lower position via a rarely used and probably unknown ford to the Federals. This location was mostly likely suggested by Captain Hugh Ramsey Thompson Koontz, who was from the area. Dulany's troops crossed the creek unopposed, but it was soon evident that the flanking movement had been observed by the Federals. As soon as Dulany's men reached the opposite bank, they were confronted by a body of New Jersey horsemen, which, though they had come too late to hold the ford, stood ready to block the way of the Confederates. Dulany ordered Captain Dan Hatcher, commanding the First Squadron of the Seventh, to charge the Federals now blocking their way. Hatcher moved forward, turned to the left and then quickly wheeled to the right, striking the Federals on the half flank just as Dulany, with the rest of his force, charged full in front. The Federals made a feeble resistance and then turned and fled up the creek, halting on a hill near their main body. Captain Frank Myers with the Thirty-fifth Battalion charged them "with pistol and sabres" and drove them back across the hill. It was probably at this time that Captain Myers was seriously wounded. With the war taking its toll on the officers of the Thirty-fifth, Lieutenant Nick Dorsey took over command of the battalion. Rosser now had a regiment and a battalion across the creek threatening the Federal left flank. Rosser ordered the regiments still remaining on the far bank to charge across the ford where the Back Road crossed Mill Creek. As the rest of the Confederate cavalry charged across the ford directly into Custer's main line, Captain Hatcher struck Custer's flank. The Federals withdrew and fell back on the rear of their trains. Rosser pursued directly up the Back Road, while other units used little-known farm paths to once again attack the Federals' flank. It was about this time that the Federals lost many of their wagons, a number of which held slaves and unionist families traveling with the Federals. According to an account of a participant, "these people were treated badly."

The rest of the gray force pursued the Federals several miles until it ran into a considerable force of Federals posted behind a rail pile at the edge of a woods not far from Columbia Furnace. The Twelfth Cavalry charged, and the Federals again retreated. Small groups of regular troops and partisans hit the Federals all the way to Columbia Furnace, where they went into camp. During the day, the Confederates lost two men killed, including Captain Hugh Ramsey Thompson Koontz. Koontz was from Mount Jackson, and his home was only about three miles from the place of his death. Captain Koontz had commanded Company K, Twelfth Virginia Cavalry Regiment, since early in the war. At Mill Creek, he commanded the regiment. According to General Rosser, Captain Koontz was mortally wounded "while gallantly leading a charge of his regiment." He commanded the regiment for less than an hour. Captain Koontz is buried in the Union Cemetery in Mount Jackson. His gave stone reads, "Recognized as a brave, determined and gallant officer."

Custer put out a double line of pickets around his camps at Columbia Furnace. The next morning, the Federals moved on north. Before leaving the Columbia Furnace, the Eighteenth Pennsylvania Cavalry burned the furnace and took up the rear of the column. Very soon, Custer's column was attacked again, although with less vigor this time.

Despite the fighting along the Back Road, Custer's burners continued their work. Just north of the village of Fairview, Custer's men reached the farm owned by Levi and Mary Gouchenour, whose son Philip was a private in White's Comanches. When the Federals set fire to the Gouchenours' barn, flying embers landed on the roof of the family's home. Gouchenour climbed up on the roof, and his wife and children handed up buckets of water, which he used to douse the hot spots. The heat on the roof singed Gouchenour's eyebrows, but he continued his work and saved the house. By the time Rosser's men reached Fairview, it was too late. A Confederate captain reported that "every home was visited, the proud mansion and the humble cottage feeling alike the blasting and savage hand of war." Skirmishing lasted most of the day until Custer neared the Valley Pike, where the fighting broke off.

Returns from Third Division regiments indicate that the Federals lost at least eight officers and sixty-three troopers killed or wounded, along with more than one hundred captured during this period, not to mention the material captured or recaptured by Rosser's men. Corporal Kiser of the Eleventh Virginia Cavalry noted with satisfaction that they had come into "contact with the Yanks giving them a pretty good threshing capturing a good many Stolen sheep…and nearly all their wagon train." What Kiser and most of the Confederates did not realize was that, once expended, the energy of man and beast could not be replenished on almost nonexistent rations. The late John Heatwole, the finest authority on "The Burning," summed up the results of this period: "The Federals were consuming all the forage that time would allow, and the rest was being carried off or destroyed. When strength would count for everything, the Southerners would be in a sorry state."

The same kind of wholesale destruction took place along both sides of the Valley Pike. All the mills along Mill Creek in Mount Jackson were burned, as were most of the barns in the area. All the outbuildings at Mount Airy were destroyed, and most of the livestock was slaughtered. From a hill near Mount Jackson, Union cavalrymen counted 168 barns burning at one time. Edinburg-area farmers lost their barns and outbuildings, as well, but both mills in town were spared. The townspeople prevailed upon Sheridan to spare the Edinburg Mill as it was being set afire. Sheridan allowed the fire to be extinguished.

A portion of the burnt timbers can be seen today at the mill, which is now a museum. Whissen Mill, farther down Stony Creek on the other end of town, was saved because a group of troopers from the Twelfth Virginia Cavalry took position on the hill above the ford leading to the mill and set up a brisk fire on the burners as they attempted to cross the creek.

The Edinburg Mill as it appeared in 1936. *Courtesy of the Edinburg Heritage Foundation.*

Whissen Mill, located in Edinburg. This mill was saved from destruction by the presence of Confederate troops on the bluff above the mill. The mill burned down in 1918.

At Woodstock, Federal troops entered the town and began laying waste to everything of possible value to the Confederates. A portion of the Nineteenth New York Cavalry destroyed the railroad depot, warehouses, a locomotive and three boxcars on the siding. Steady winds came up and accidently ignited fires in buildings on the outskirts of town. Federal soldiers

Fisher's Mill, in the village of Fisher's Hill. This mill was not burned in 1864, but its equipment was seriously damaged.

helped to extinguish those fires. That evening, Sheridan sent a telegram to Grant from Woodstock reporting that the destruction of the valley had reached from mountain to mountain in Augusta County to the south and would continue the next day to Strasburg in the north. When it was all over, Sheridan's men had systematically destroyed about 1,400 barns, countless other farm structures, seventy mills, several factories, three iron furnaces, warehouses and railroad buildings and hundreds of thousands of bushels of wheat, oats and corn, as well as crops standing in the fields. Valley residents who complained about the wholesale destruction were told, per Sheridan's instructions, "that they have furnished too many meals to guerrillas to expect much sympathy."

After fighting with Custer's rear guard all day, Rosser went into camp near Spiker's Hill on the evening of October 8. Custer's division bivouacked northeast of Mount Olive on the Back Road. To the east, Lomax's Division bivouacked on both sides of the Valley Pike behind Jordon Run, just south of Tom's Brook. Opposing him was Brigadier General Wesley Merritt's division encamped at the base of Round Hill. The two Federal cavalry

The field along the Back Road near Tom's Brook where General Custer maneuvered for his attack against Rosser's troopers.

divisions were under the overall command of Brigadier General Alfred Torbert, Sheridan's chief of cavalry. Sheridan was upset with Rosser's conduct along the Back Road and Torbert's timid response. Bursting into Torbert's quarters, Sheridan ordered Torbert to move at daylight and "whip the rebel cavalry or get whipped himself."

At dawn on October 9, both Custer and Merritt attacked the two wings of the Confederate cavalry. Merritt's 3,500 Yankees overwhelmed General Lunsford Lomax's 1,500 poorly armed troopers, but Custer had more difficulty. His 2,500 men faced 2,000 men under the command of Rosser, who was, coincidentally, a close friend of Custer's at West Point before the war. Rosser placed Colonel Thomas T. Munford's troops on his left, straddling the Back Road. Other units and artillery were spread out along the Confederate center and right.

They were just south of Tom's Brook. Lunsford Lomax's 1,500-man brigade faced Wesley Merritt's division along the Valley Pike.

Rosser's defensive position was too strong for a frontal assault, and defective artillery shells hindered the reduction of the position. Custer

Spiker's Hill on the Tom's Brook Battlefield. This was the location of the Confederate artillery opposing Custer's forces on October 9, 1864.

decided that he would need to maneuver around the enemy position in order to break the impasse.

He ordered three of his regiments to turn the Confederate left flank. When Munford reported this movement to Rosser, he made light of it, exclaiming that he would drive the Federals back to Strasburg. But on their second attempt, the Federal troopers succeeded in turning the Confederate flank. From left to right, Rosser's position crumbled, and his troops started to flee the field. Over on the Valley Pike, Merritt's troops flanked Lomax on his left and forced his men to abandon their position.

Rosser's men scattered and ran for twenty miles while Lomax's men unsuccessfully tried to halt the Federal advance along the pike, losing artillery on each attempt. The assault ended only when the Confederates reached Early's infantry lines at Mount Jackson. The Federal troops captured eleven guns, plus Rosser's wagons, desk and papers. They even took his overcoat. The Confederates also lost about 350 men killed, wounded or captured. It was said that Munford never forgave Rosser for the rout at Tom's Brook and never spoke to him again. The Battle

Round Hill was used by both sides as a signal station during several periods. It was from here that Sheridan observed the Battle of Tom's Brook.

of Tom's Brook came to be called, derisively, "The Woodstock Races." Nine Union troopers were killed, and forty-eight were wounded. Sheridan watched the battle form Round Hill.

Sheridan continued his withdrawal the next day. Leaving Strasburg, his infantry retired to the north banks of Cedar Creek. The Sixth Corps continued the march and turned east at Middletown, marching by way of Front Royal on its way to join Grant at Richmond. Rosser's cavalrymen again followed Sheridan's withdrawal, though not nearly as recklessly as before. When they reached the site of the disaster at Tom's Brook, they spent some time opening the hastily dug graves searching for friends or relatives killed in the fight. Rosser's scouts soon advised Early of the departure of the Federal Sixth Corps, forcing him to show his hand. He knew the only way he could keep that corps from joining Grant was to reestablish contact and again threaten offensive action.

On October 13, Early reoccupied Fisher's Hill and pushed through Strasburg to Hupp's Hill, where he engaged a portion of Sheridan's army at the Stickley farm. When Sheridan realized the proximity of Early's forces,

The remains of earthworks dug by Federal forces in 1864.

he recalled the Sixth Corps. Sheridan left the area to attend a conference in Washington and was in Winchester, fourteen miles north of his army, when fighting began on the morning of October 19.

That left General Wright in charge of the army. He was convinced that his left flank was protected by the North Fork of the Shenandoah River, so he concentrated his efforts on protecting his right, where he expected an attack to come. He was wrong. The Confederates knew the valley well, and on the night of October 19, they marched around the Federal left. Early that morning, the Confederates launched their attack.

The attack was an immediate and spectacular success. The Federal Eighth Corps was hit first and retreated in chaos. Next was the Nineteenth Corps, which was also pushed out of its camp, although in slightly better condition. Finally, the Sixth Corps was forced back by the Confederate rush, although this time in reasonably good order. By midmorning, most of Early's men thought they had won a great victory.

This was when Early's day started to go sour. The Federal Sixth Corps was able to form a strong line north of the battlefield. Elements of the Nineteenth Corps began to form around them, and by 10:30 a.m., this new line was probably too strong for Early's men to attack with any chance of success. At the same time, many of the Confederate soldiers had begun to loot the Union camps. Early was later blamed this for his eventual defeat.

Worse was yet to come. Sheridan had been alerted by the sound of artillery from the south. At first, he dismissed it as too light to indicate a battle, but he soon changed his mind and began what was to become his famous ride from Winchester. Just south of Winchester, Sheridan found the first evidence of the disaster at Cedar Creek—fleeing men, mostly of the Eighth Corps, desperate to get to safety. Riding south, he rallied as many men as he could, stopping whenever he encountered a large group of retreating soldiers to encourage them to turn south. Reaching the new Union line at about 10:30 a.m., he helped to stop the retreat. Over the next five hours, Sheridan reorganized his shattered army in preparation for a counterattack. That counterattack came at four o'clock in the afternoon. Early's men briefly held but broke under the Federal attack and fled from the field. Once again, Sheridan suffered more losses than Early, but once again he could afford to. Early lost 320 dead, 1,540 wounded, 1,050 missing and captured, 43 guns and most of his supplies—perhaps as much as one-third of his entire force. Sheridan's men lost 644 dead, 3,430 wounded and 1,591 missing and wounded, demonstrating the ferocity of the fighting. Even so, that still

Spengler's Mill at Strasburg. It was here that Custer captured a great deal of Confederate equipment following the Battle of Cedar Creek. The mill was spared from destruction in 1864.

left Sheridan outnumbering Early by as many as five to one. The Battle of Cedar Creek in 1864 marked the end of Confederate dominion over the Shenandoah Valley. It also marked the end and of the war-weariness that had plagued the North.

Despite his defeat, Early and the Confederates did not flee the valley. While Sheridan spent the winter at Kernstown, Early camped at New Market. Sheridan was finally able to dispatch most of his infantry to the Petersburg front, keeping only his cavalry and a few scattered units in the valley. The fight for control of the Shenandoah Valley was over as far as important operations were concerned. More fighting and dying would take place, and the population would endure more suffering, but the valley would be of no more value to the Confederacy.

General Early attempted one last ill-conceived and poorly executed offensive on November 11, when he advanced to Middletown and Ninevah. Torbert and the Yankee cavalry crushed the Confederates at Newtown and Ninevah, forcing Early to withdraw his infantry and return to Rude's Hill. The next day, General Lee directed Early to transfer as many troops as possible to Richmond.

Over the next several days, the few men left under Early's command were moved around from location to location. The cavalry moved about from place to place. Forage for the horses was almost nonexistent, and food for the troops was growing scarce. By mid-November, the weather had become intensely cold, with the wind whipping the snow into blizzard-like conditions. The mountains were already white.

On November 22, Sheridan sent Torbert, along with Powell's and Custer's cavalries, on a reconnaissance to ascertain the remaining strength of Early's army. Powell's Second Division, taking the lead, ran into Early's cavalry pickets, driving them through Mount Jackson to the Confederate infantry lines at Rude's Hill. Some of the Federal horsemen stopped at the Confederate hospital, where "their medical officers came into the hospital and acted very uncivilly, requiring a list of all officers, saying they would remove all on their return…they carried off with them some bedding…and clothing of a portion of the wounded."

As the Federal cavalry began to appear on the north side of North Fork, Early ordered out his infantry and placed his artillery on the crest of Rude's Hill, where they began shelling the Federals. Despite the shelling, the Federal cavalry advanced across most of Meem's Bottoms, taking a considerable loss and retiring in disorder. Custer's men covered the Federal retreat, which was pursued with infantry to Hawkinstown and with cavalry as far Edinburg. As winter came, Early's little army moved farther south, but Rosser remained in the county. Rosser's main camps were near Timberville, and it was from these camps that Rosser led two successful raids into West Virginia. On one raid, they succeeded in capturing the entire garrison at New Creek, along with many supplies and horses. Along their return route, they gathered livestock, returning to Timberville on December 2 with nearly five hundred head of cattle. Even with these new supplies, the Confederate cavalry was unable to provide fodder for the horses.

In mid-December, Custer and most of his division made one more trek through the county as they passed through on a raid toward Staunton. Icy roads caused Custer to halt at Lacey's Springs and go into camp. Rosser followed with a skeleton cavalry force, surprising Custer with a night attack on his camp. The Confederates overran the camps, but little real damage was caused. Custer then returned to Winchester, where he spent the winter with his wife.

WINTER FOR THE RESIDENTS

By the winter of 1864–65, the people of Shenandoah County must have felt beaten, if not cowed, and were certainly impoverished and near starvation. With the Federals now seemingly content to hole up in their camps in Fredrick County, many from the Laurel Brigade were allowed to go to their homes for the winter because the Confederate government was no longer able to feed them or their horses. As the miseries of the men multiplied, a feeling of hopelessness grew, and the number of desertions increased proportionately. Even the lauded Seventh Virginia Cavalry was dispersed, with only Company C remaining together for the rest of the winter, which it spent in Fort Valley. By the time Rosser attempted his next foray in January, his force was at less than 40 percent of its former strength.

The desolation in the Lower Shenandoah Valley was so great that General Sheridan felt it necessary to issue rations to those persons most in need. Late in January, he advised the authorities at U.S. Army Headquarters in Washington City that he had already issued rations to nearly eight hundred residents and notified them that he expected that number to increase. In that notification, he requested official permission for his actions, which drew a quick and sharp reply from chief of staff Major General Henry W. Halleck:

It is within the authority of a commanding officer to afford temporary relief to those whom the fortunes of war have placed in his hand or under his immediate protection, but no authority can be given for the subsistence of rebel families outside of our lines, nor even within, any longer than till they can be removed or sent to their friends and natural protectors. The disloyal people of the Shenandoah south of Winchester and outside of our lines have been and are now, at full liberty to join friends in the rebel service… The disloyal within our lines should be sent South to feed upon the enemy. Loyal refugees should be temporarily assisted and sent North where they can earn a livelihood, While the men of Virginia are either serving in the rebel ranks, or, as bushwhackers, are waylaying and murdering our soldiers, our Government must decline to support their wives and children.

Sheridan began to take a harsher line when he realized that all the pleas for help were not genuine. He cited an example concerning George A. Hupp, who lived near Strasburg: "I issued to him thirty days' rations, and afterward found that he had six months' supplies buried; two sons in the rebel army…$10,000 in gold under his floor, and a sword that belonged to Stonewall Jackson."

At dawn on February 27, 1865, Sheridan and his cavalry broke camp at Winchester and headed south. Along with two full cavalry divisions and a section of artillery, the blue-clad force included a long train of supply wagons, a pontoon train and two medical wagons. Spies in Winchester and soldiers manning the Confederate signal station on Massanutten Mountain had already detected signs of the impending Union movement. The blue column moved up the Valley Pike on the twenty-seventh, stopping to camp for the night at Woodstock. The next morning, with Custer's Third Division in the lead, the march resumed. At Mount Jackson, eight troopers drowned while attempting to swim their horses across the rain-swollen North Fork of the Shenandoah River. "[M]any others would have been drowned had it not been for the superhuman efforts of a number of officers and men… who rushed into the stream, and at great personal risk brought them to the shore," reported the commander of Custer's First Brigade, Colonel Alexander Pennington. The rest of the army waited for the engineers to put out a preconstructed pontoon bridge.

Sheridan arrived at Staunton and then turned east where Custer's division defeated the remnant of Early's army at Waynesboro on March 2. Early and a few of his staff managed to escape, but 1,500 the men were captured. This marked the end of the Army of the Valley, as well as the end of Jubal Early's military career.

Colonel John L. Thompson, commanding a combined force consisting of the First New Hampshire Cavalry, the First Rhode Island Cavalry and the Twenty-second New York Cavalry, was tasked with escorting the almost 1,500 Confederate prisoners back down the Valley Pike to the railhead at Stephenson's Depot. Thompson marched first to Staunton, where food was secured from the asylum for the three-day trip north. The weather was wet and cold as the caravan moved north.

General Rosser, collecting his scattered command—many of whom had been furloughed for the winter—ordered a general rendezvous at Mount Jackson, the point where the North Fork crosses the road. Thompson and the prisoners arrived at Meem's Bottoms just south of the North Fork about noon on March 6 and found the fords held by Confederates who were digging in along the far bank. A number of Confederate troops were also following in Thompson's rear. The river was not fordable except at a single point, which was too strongly held to be forced. Thompson settled in for the evening, ordering that the prisoners be held in the fields of Meem's Bottoms.

The following morning, the river had fallen to a point where it was fordable. Thompson ordered the First Rhode Island to charge the ford. The Federal cavalrymen plunged into the water and drove the Confederates from the far bank, capturing a number of additional prisoners in the process. At the same time, the Federals were forcing the crossing of the North Fork. Rosser, with about three hundred men, made several desperate but unsuccessful charges at Rude's Hill on the First New Hampshire, which was acting as the rear guard. The Confederates suffered some loss in killed and captured at this time.

The prisoners forded the river in parties of fifty, each party forming a body in the shape of a wedge, with the point upstream and each man firmly holding his neighbor by the arm. The stream was breast high and running rapidly; single persons would have been swept away. The column reached Winchester, where the prisoners were loaded onto to trains and taken to prison camps in the North.

Sheridan's supply trains and cavalry patrols were constantly confronted by bushwhackers, so he created a band of special scouts under the command of Major Henry H. Young of his staff. Young's earlier exploits with the Second Rhode Island Infantry had resulted in his promotion from the rank of lieutenant to the eventual inclusion as a member of Sheridan's staff. Young's scouts often dressed in Confederate uniforms and claimed to be "a body of recruits for Gilmore coming from Maryland and pursued by the Yankee Cavalry." Every day, these scouts scoured the valley looking for bushwhackers and reporting to headquarters concerning the state of affairs. On December 12, 1864, Young's men caught up with Levi Crabill, a suspected bushwhacker, near Strasburg, and when he tried to escape, he was shot in the back and died later the night.

On January 19, 1865, Young, with about twenty scouts dressed as Confederate soldiers, left Winchester on an intelligence mission. Trailing Young was a fifty-man support detachment from the Fifth New York Cavalry. After entering Shenandoah County, Young left the New Yorkers at Maurertown and rode to Edinburg under the disguised mission of returning the body of a local Confederate for proper burial. Captain George Grandstaff, commander of Company E, Twelfth Virginia Cavalry, was suspicious of the unrecognized Southerners and invited their leader to dinner at the Ritter home at the north end of town. Young was able to determine the strength of the Confederate garrison and returned to Maurertown, where he rejoined the New Yorkers and went into camp.

Just after dawn on the twenty-second, Young's men returned to Edinburg, where they captured Lieutenant Monroe Funkhouser and fifteen Confederate soldiers. Young's party headed north, but despite the advice from some of his men, Young insisted on stopping at Woodstock for breakfast. Back in Edinburg, Grandstaff and Lieutenant Joseph Miley assembled a few men and headed after Young, picking up additional men as they went. By the time Grandstaff reached Woodstock, he had gathered a force numbering nearly twenty.

According to the Federal account of this action, a one-armed butcher who was a unionist tipped Young off that about three hundred Confederate cavalrymen were closing in on the town. The Federals managed to get out of town ahead of the Confederates. Whether it was simple panic in the mind of the butcher or a simple overestimate on the part of the Federals, the Confederates could not have had anything approaching three hundred men.

Very early that same morning, north of Woodstock, Silas Wright, also from Grandstaff's company, saw the New York troopers en route to Woodstock. Wright spread the alarm and assembled about fourteen of his comrades from their homes in the Maurertown area. By eight o'clock that morning, Wight's group, commanded by Captain Martin Strickler, hid in Koontz's woods just north of Pugh's Run, where they waited for the returning Federal party. Strickler allowed most of the Federals to cross the bridge and then charged into the rear guard. In the early moments of the mêlée, sixteen-year-old George Bushong from Tom's Brook was mortally wounded. Just south of the bridge, Colonel Young's horse was shot from under him, and he was almost captured. Two scouts returned, and Young jumped on the back of one of the scout's horses. About this time, Captain Grandstaff arrived and assumed command, and the pursuit continued. The Federals made a brief stand in Maurertown, where several prisoners were captured and taken to Edinburg. The next attempt to end the pursuit was made by the Federals at the "Four-Mile House," south of Strasburg. According to S.K. Write in his article appearing in the April 1921 edition of the *Confederate Veteran*:

> *All that was needed here were a few shots and the old Confed's battle yell, and they broke into one of the wildest, craziest stampedes that I have ever witnessed. We rode through them and over them. They actually jumped off their mounts and tried to outrun them. At Fisher's Hill eight or ten of them jumped over the stone wall, fifteen or twenty feet high, and crept under the cedar brush on the other side. The boys dragged them out by their legs. About three hundred yards north of the stone bridge at Fisher's Hill we recaptured the last prisoner and ceased the pursuit in the suburbs of Strasburg.*

The Confederates recovered all their men, killed at least one of the scouts, mortally wounded two others and captured four others, including Thomas Cassidy, who was dressed in a Confederate uniform. Approximately ten of the accompanying New York troopers were also captured, along with twenty horses. Sheridan knew that a Yankee captured in a Confederate uniform would likely be executed, so he sent staff officer Major Philip Baird, under a flag of truce, to Woodstock with an offer of a prisoner exchange. At Woodstock, Baird met with Captain Grandstaff, erroneously referred to in a Federal account as a major from the Seventeenth Virginia Cavalry, and proposed the exchange. Baird was accompanied by a uniformed escort, which included at least one of the scouts from the earlier raid. While Baird and Grandstaff met, a woman in the crowd watching the proceeding recognized the scout and pointed him out. Several people in the crowd began to stir, and the meeting was ended without the exchange. Cassidy was never exchanged, and his body was never located.

CONFEDERATE SIGNAL CORPS INFORMATION

During early February, the ranking Confederate signal corpsman, Master Sergeant S.A. Dunning, abandoned his post atop Three-Top Mountain and turned himself into the Federals. Dunning provided a wealth of information about the signal system and the state of affairs in the area, some of which later appeared in the *Official Records*:

> *We had a very fine glass (captured from the Federal Army), with which we could look into the streets of Winchester. No force can leave Winchester or go to Strasburg, Front Royal, Ashby's Gap, or Snicker's Gap, or in any direction, without being seen, except at night or rainy weather. We were on post from 8 a.m. until 3 p.m. Usually we boarded with Mr. Braush Mackintosh, near the signal station...There is a chain of signal stations, all connecting with New Market, from which place a telegraph goes to General Early's headquarters. There is a station on the mountain at Ashby's Gap; one at hominy Hollow, on Bock's Hill, near Front Royal; one at Burnt Springs, on Fort Mountain, opposite Honeyville; at Ed. Browman's, between Burnt Springs and New Market Gap, and the station at Pitman Point (Three-Top Mountain near Strasburg)...There is a picket post of three companies at Edenburg [sic]. The furnace in Fort Valley, about eight miles from Edenburg, is working for the government; no guard there...The stages run daily between Mount Jackson and Staunton...The citizens in the Valley are very destitute, and depend principally on their friends south of Staunton.*

There appears to have been about two dozen men in the signal detachment operating at Signal Knob, and they usually worked in three shifts daily. When not on duty, the men lived in a hotel at Burner's Springs. The Warren County Historical Society has the hotel register wherein the proprietor kept an account of these troops for reimbursement from the Confederate government. The Confederate signal operation on the Massanutten was an excellent example of a fully integrated intelligence-gathering and communications system making use of both visual signaling and telegraph.

DESTRUCTION OF ELIZABETH FURNACE

Based on the information Sergeant Dunning supplied, Sheridan realized there were few if any Confederates left in Fort Valley to protect the ironworks at Elizabeth Furnace. Since the furnace was still in semioperational order, Sheridan decided to brave the icy roads and destroy the furnace. On February 13, Lieutenant Colonel George R. Maxwell and three hundred troopers from the First Michigan Cavalry left Winchester, traveled up the Valley Pike and approached Edinburg in an attempt to capture the Stony Creek picket. The natural defenses afforded by Stony Creek made Edinburg a favored location to place Confederate picket posts throughout much of the war. Picketing troops, unless they lived in the area, were normally billeted with signal troops on Humston Hill south of town. With the approach of Maxwell's men, the pickets withdrew. Maxwell stayed with about two hundred men in Edinburg, while the other troops crossed Edinburg Gap into Powell's Fort Valley and moved to Elizabeth Furnace. At the furnace, the Federals captured ten men—five soldiers and five detailed men—and damaged the furnace to the point where it could no longer be operated.

The Confederate pickets south of Edinburg constantly waited for a chance to attack Maxwell and finally decided to do so as he withdrew from the town on the morning of the sixteenth. As the column got underway, the rear guard was charged by about fifty men of the Twelfth Virginia Cavalry, who were repulsed. A constant skirmish was kept up on the Federal rear guard until they reached Woodstock. At Woodstock, the Confederates tried to charge the column but were driven back, "as they could not complete with our superior carbine...The enemy suffered severely in this encounter," according to Maxwell's report. At Tom's Brook, Maxwell halted his column and charged the Confederates, driving them back toward Edinburg. Maxwell then moved down Valley Pike "unmolested save by a few partisans near Strasburg." As Federals reached Cedar Creek, they were joined by the force sent to destroy Elizabeth Furnace. Maxwell reported the loss of one man mortally wounded, while the Confederates suffered "three of the enemy killed and a number wounded; ten men captured; twenty horses captured."

THE FINAL ACTIONS IN THE VALLEY

On March 20, Captain William Oliver led a troop of the Fourth New York Cavalry by a circuitous route to Woodstock and then up the Valley Pike to Edinburg, where they captured a captain of the Twelfth Virginia Cavalry and two other soldiers. On his return, he was ambushed at Fisher's Hill by a party of Confederates who quickly retired in the face of superior manpower. Still another detachment left Winchester on March 2, scouted as far south as Woodstock and returned unmolested, other than a brief skirmish at Newtown.

Near the beginning of April, Colonel Charles T. O'Ferrall, with a small troop from the Twenty-third Virginia Cavalry, was camped at Paintertown north of Edinburg when he received a message from the Confederate signal station on Signal Knob about the advance of some four hundred Federal troopers. O'Ferrall dispatched scouts to keep him informed of the whereabouts of the Federal column. Late that same night, he received word that the Federal column was camped at Pugh's Run north of Woodstock. O'Ferrall led his men north toward the Federal encampment. O'Ferrall dismounted his men and proceeded on foot to within one hundred feet of the Federal camp and then ordered a charge. He wrote what happened next:

> *The surprise was complete. In the shortest time imaginable the whole force, except the prisoners, and we had four or five each, were running for dear life in every direction. No twenty-eight men in the world ever made more noise or did more shooting in such a short time. We were loaded down with pistols and carbines, which we had captured, and we kept up a perfect fusillade, at the same time my bugler…was, as I had directed him, sounding the cavalry charge with all the lung power his Maker had given him, making the impression that our numbers were large.*

The badly shaken Federals quickly scattered, leaving their camp to the Southerners. The Southerners captured a number of prisoners, along with many badly needed horses, while losing only one man wounded.

The Federals did not venture back into their abandoned camps until after daylight. Regrouping, they cautiously proceeded on to Woodstock, where they did an about-face and headed back to the safety of Winchester.

Because of the success of O'Ferrall's raid, General Torbert, with some 3,500 men, moved from Winchester to Mount Jackson, forcing O'Ferrall to shift his main camp to New Market. Once Torbert retired, O'Ferrall's scouts followed and attacked his rear guard near Woodstock, capturing several prisoners. Of his actions in early April, O'Ferrall wrote:

> *And now I come to make the claim that it was upon the soil of Shenandoah County that the last Confederate line was held, the last fight made, and the last prisoner captured by any part of the Army of Northern Virginia. I make the further claim that my little command held the last Confederate line, made the last fight, and captured the last prisoner held, made and captured upon the soil of old Virginia.*

O'Farrell's claims mattered little, though, for the end had come two days earlier at Appomattox when General Lee officially surrendered the Army of Northern Virginia. News of the surrender reached O'Ferrall at New Market on Friday, April 14. O'Ferrall received a dispatch from General Lomax authorizing him to surrender or disband. O'Ferrall gave a stirring speech to his men and declared the regiment disbanded. He also told his men that he intended to join Johnston's forces still fighting in North Carolina. That evening, O'Ferrall and about thirty of his men left New Market. Johnston's surrender took place shortly thereafter, and O'Ferrall finally disbanded his group somewhere between Staunton and Lynchburg.

9

Surrender and Return
of the Soldiers

On April 1, General Grant finally broke General Lee's lines and forced Lee out of his entrenchments at Petersburg. On April 2, Lee informed Jefferson Davis that Petersburg and Richmond would have to be evacuated. Lee's army headed southwest, but Grant aggressively blocked Lee's every move. Grant finally cornered Lee at Appomattox Court House. Out of options, Lee surrendered his Army of Northern Virginia on April 9, 1865.

The terms of surrender were generous: Officers and men could go home "not to be disturbed by U.S. authority so long as they observe their paroles and the laws in force where they may reside." Cavalrymen were allowed to keep their horses since they were personally owned by the men. Officers were allowed to keep their sidearms and swords. The formal surrender took place the following day, and individual paroles were issued to all Confederates who were present at the surrender. Valley soldiers not present for the surrender were required to report to Winchester or other designated places to obtain their patrols. The chief parole officer late reported that "a great many others have been paroled by my advance cavalry at Strasburg, Woodstock, and New Market...embracing the small commands in that section of country."

Each man's parole bore his name and the name of his company and regiment and recorded his pledge to fight no more until he was regularly exchanged. Former Confederates between the ages of eighteen and thirty-five were required to carry their paroles in their pocket and present them to proper authorities when requested. Many Confederates proudly preserved their paroles as proof of the fact that they were in the fight to the last.

By the time O'Ferrall disbanded his followers, valley soldiers were already reaching their homes after the journey from Appomattox. By now, little remained of the valley regiments that had marched off to war in 1861. When the surrender finally came at Appomattox, fewer than twenty men of the Thirty-third Virginia Infantry were present to lay down their arms. The generosity of Grant's surrender terms at Appomattox and the sympathetic attitude of most Union soldiers present at the surrender helped in some ways to ease the pain of the Confederates.

There is a certain respect between fighting men, even though they might be on opposing sides. Unfortunately, occupation forces were seldom combat veterans, so they generally did not share the mutual respect among combat veterans. A good example of this situation is the 192nd Ohio Infantry, the regiment assigned to the main Federal occupation camp in Shenandoah County located at Rude's Hill. The 192nd was mustered in for one year's service on March 9, 1865, under the command of Colonel Francis W. Butterfield. Unlike his men, Butterfield had seen three years of real military experience as a captain in the 8th Ohio Volunteer Infantry. Butterfield's deputy, Lieutenant Colonel Cyrus Hussey, had also been in the army before joining the 192nd, but unlike Butterfield, Hussey's service had consisted of staff duty. The first task of the 192nd was to dismantle the buildings of the Confederate hospital at Mount Jackson and move the building material to Rude's Hill, where it constructed its camp. The entire regiment was at Rude's Hill except for two companies stationed in Harrisonburg.

Captain George W. Summers and Sergeant Newton Koontz, formerly of Company D, Seventh Virginia Cavalry, together with two other men from their old unit, left their homes in Page County en route to Rude's Hill to obtain their paroles. Somewhere along the route, they encountered a group of men from the Twenty-second New York Cavalry. An argument led to an altercation that resulted in the Confederates taking several horses at gunpoint. Upon their return home with their captured goods, Captain Summers's father induced several prominent citizens from Page County to journey to Rude's Hill in an effort to straighten out the affair. Colonel Butterfield advised these men that the return of the captured goods would close the issue. The horses were returned, and Colonel Butterfield issued a receipt for the returned property.

A short time later, Summers became involved in an argument with a local man named William Tharp. Tharp threatened to seek revenge for the Federals at Rude's Hill. Two days later, a party of Federals went to Page County, arrested both Summers and Koontz and escorted them to Rude's

Hill, where they were told of their pending execution. The two men learned that Colonel Butterfield was on leave, and Lieutenant Colonel Hussey, a perennial "staff wiener," was now in command. The two men freely admitted their guilt and pleaded for their lives, but to no avail. A short distance from the camp, the men were placed on their knees, tied to stakes and shot. The actual spot of the execution, almost directly opposite Cedar Grove Church, was initially marked with only a simple locust post. In 1893, Captain Jack Adams and others placed a marble monument on the spot that is still visible from the Valley Pike. Some years later, Captain Jack Adams was able to gather the funds to build the marble obelisk that stand at the location today.

The Summers-Koontz Monument at Rude's Hill.

Holly Circle at the Massanutten Cemetery in Woodstock, Virginia. Here the people of the county reinterred soldiers removed from other parts of the county.

Conclusion

The war destroyed at least half of the assessed wealth in Shenandoah County. The railroad, which had held so much promise five years earlier, was completely destroyed. The Valley Pike, which had improved the lives of so many, was now severely damaged.

The production of wheat, the crop on which much of the economy depended, was gone. The crops of 1864 were taken by the completing armies or burned in the barns. The prospects of a new crop for 1865 were bleak. Horses to pull the plows had died or been stolen; the farm machinery had been wrecked; the fields, left unattended in the last year of the war, were full of weeds; and fences no longer existed to keep the few livestock left out of the field. Barns and corncribs used to store crops had been burned, and most of the mills used to grind the grain had been damaged or destroyed. Worst of all, many of the finest sons of Shenandoah County rested in shallow graves in hundreds of fields across Virginia, Pennsylvania and Maryland. Many others had returned home with missing limbs or chronic diseases that would shorten their lives.

But Shenandoah County would rebound. The people were resilient, hardworking and determined. The railroad was rebuilt, the roads repaired and the fields were planted. Shenandoah County over next few decades once again to become "the land of milk and honey." The citizens never forgot the war and took great pains to honor their fallen. Confederate bodies quickly buried throughout the county were moved to cemeteries, where they would forever be honored.

Bibliography

Alexandria Gazette. Microfilm. Prince William Public Library, Alexandria, Virginia.

Anderson, Paul Christopher. *Blood Image: Turner Ashby in the Civil War and the Southern Mind*. Baton Rouge: Louisiana State University Press, 2002.

Armstrong, Richard L. *11th Virginia Cavalry*. Lynchburg, VA: H.E. Howard, Inc., 1989.

Avirett, James B. *The Memoirs of General Turner Ashby and His Compeers*. Baltimore, MD: Selby and Dulany, 1867.

Ayers, Edward L. *In the Presence of Mine Enemies: War in the Heart of America, 1859–1863*. New York: Norton, 2003.

Ballard, Charles. "Dismissing the Peculiar Institution: Assessing Slavery in Page and Rockingham Counties, Virginia." Paper presented to the Shenandoah Valley Regional Studies Seminar, James Madison University, Harrisonburg, Virginia, April 17, 1998.

Bean, W.G. *Stonewall's Man Sandie Pendleton*. Chapel Hill: University of North Carolina Press, 1959.

Benedict, G.G. *Vermont in the Civil War: A History of the Part Taken by the Vermont Soldiers and Sailors in the War for the Union.* 2 vols. Burlington, VT: Free Press Association, 1886.

Black, Robert C. *The Railroads of the Confederacy.* Chapel Hill: University of North Carolina Press, 1952.

Brice, Marshall M. *Conquest of a Valley.* Verona, VA: McClure Printing Company, Inc., 1974.

Brown, Kent Masterson. *Retreat from Gettysburg: Lee, Logistics, & the Pennsylvania Campaign.* Chapel Hill: University of North Carolina Press, 2005.

Bushong, Millard K., and Dean M. Bushong. *Fightin' Tom Rosser, C.S.A.* Shippensburg, PA: Biedel Printing House, Inc., 1983.

Casler, John O. *Four Years in the Stonewall Brigade.* Dayton, OH: Morningside Bookshop, 1992.

Clark, Champ. *Decoying the Yankees: Jackson's Valley Campaign.* Alexandria, VA: Time-Life Books, Inc., 1984.

Clinton, Catherine, ed. *Southern Families at War: Loyalty and Conflict in the Civil War South.* New York: Oxford University Press, 2000.

Colt, Margaretta Barton. *Defend the Valley: A Shenandoah Family in the Civil War.* New York: Crown, 1994.

Confederate Veteran. 40 vols., 1893–32.

Cooke, John Esten. *Wearing of Tile Gray.* Reprint ed. Gaithersburg, MD: Aide Soldier Books, Inc., 1988.

Cooling, B.F. *Jubal Early's Raid on Washington, 1864.* Baltimore, MD: Nautical & Aviation Publishing Company of America, Inc., 1989.

Couper, William. *History of the Shenandoah Valley.* Vol. 2. New York: Lewis Historical Publishing Company, Inc., 1952.

Cozzens, Peter. *Shenandoah, 1862: Stonewall Jackson's Valley Campaign*. Chapel Hill: University of North Carolina Press, 2008.

Crofts, Daniel W. *Reluctant Confederates: Upper South Unionists in the Secession Crisis*. Chapel Hill: University of North Carolina Press, 1989.

Cunningham, H.H. *Doctors in Gray: The Confederate Medical Service*. Baton Rouge: Louisiana State University Press, 1993.

Davis, Major George B., et al. *The Official Military Atlas of the Civil War*. Washington, D.C.: Government Printing Office, 1895.

Davis, William C. *The Battle of New Market*. Garden City, NY: Doubleday & Company, Inc., 1975.

De Forrest, John William. *A Volunteer's Adventures: A Unit Captain's Record of the Civil War*. New Haven, CT: Yale University Press, 1946. Reprint, Archon Books, 1970.

Delauter, Roger U., Jr. *18th Virginia Cavalry*. Lynchburg, VA: H.E. Howard, Inc., 1985.

————. *McNeill's Rangers*. Lynchburg, VA: H.E. Howard, Inc., 1986.

Divine, John E. *35th Battalion Virginia Cavalry*. Lynchburg, VA: H.E. Howard, Inc., 1985.

Douglas, Henry Kyd. *I Rode with Stonewall*. Chapel Hill: University of North Carolina Press, 1940.

DuPont, H.A. *The Campaign of 1864 in the Valley of Virginia and the Expedition to Lynchburg*. New York: National Americana Society, 1925.

Early, Jubal Anderson. *War Memoirs: Autobiographical Sketch and Narrative of the War Between the States*. Bloomington: Indiana University Press, 1960.

Ecelbarger, Gary L. *We Are in For It: The First Battle of Kernstown, March 2, 1862*. Shippensburg, PA: White Mane Publishing Co., Inc., 1997.

Freeman, Douglas Southall. *Lee's Lieutenants: A Study in Command.* Reprint ed. New York: Charles Scribner's Sons, 1970.

Frye, Dennis E. *12th Virginia Cavalry.* Lynchburg, VA: H.E. Howard, Inc., 1988.

Gallagher, Gary W. *Stephen Dodson Ramseur: Lee's Gallant General.* Chapel Hill: University of North Carolina Press, 1985.

Gallagher, Gary W., ed. *The Shenandoah Valley Campaign of 1864.* Chapel Hill: University of North Carolina Press, 2006.

———. *The Shenandoah Valley Campaign of 1862.* Chapel Hill: University of North Carolina Press, 2003

Gilmor, Harry. *Four Years in the Saddle.* Reprint ed. Baltimore, MD: Butternut and Blue, 1868

Gilmore, William. *On Hazardous Service Scouts and Spies of the North and South.* New York: Harper & Brothers, 1912.

Goff, Richard. *Confederate Supply.* Durham, NC: Duke University Press, 1969.

Good, William A. *Shadowed by the Massanutten.* Stephens City, VA: Commercial Press, Inc., 1992.

Gordon, General John B. *Reminiscences of the Civil War.* Gettysburg, PA: Civil War Times Illustrated, 1974.

Grimsley, Mark. *The Hard Hand of War: Union Military Policy toward Southern Civilians, 1861–1865.* Cambridge, UK: Cambridge University Press, 1995.

Hale, Laura Virginia. *Four Valiant Years in the Lower Shenandoah Valley, 1861–1865.* Strasburg, VA: Shenandoah Publishing House, Inc., 1968.

Hardwick, Kevin R. "After the Backcountry: Rural Life in the Great Valley of Virginia, 1800–1900." *Journal of Southern History* 68 (2002): 34–37.

Heatwole, John L. *The Burning: Sheridan in the Shenandoah Valley.* Charlottesville, VA: Rockbridge Publishing, 1998.

Henderson, George F.R. *Stonewall Jackson and the American Civil War*. Gloucester, MA: Peter Smith, 1968.

Hennessy, John. *The First Battle of Manassas: An End to Innocence, July 18–21, 1861*. Lynchburg: H.E. Howard, and Company, 1989.

Hillman, Benjamin J. *Virginia's Decision: The Story of the Secession Convention of 1861*. Richmond: Virginia Civil War Commission, 1964.

Horst, Samuel. *Mennonites in the Confederacy: A Study of Civil War Pacifism*. Scottdale, PA: Herald Press, 1967.

Hungerford, Edward. *The Story of the Baltimore & Ohio Railroad*. New York: G.P. Putnam's Sons, 1928.

Johnston, Angus James, II. *Virginia Railroads in the Civil War*. Chapel Hill: University of North Carolina Press, 1961.

Keifer, Joseph Warren. *Slavery and Four Years of War: A Political History of Slavery in the United States, Together with a Narrative of the Campaigns and Battles of the Civil War in which the Author Took Part: 1861–1865*. New York: Knickerbocker Press, 1900.

Kercheval, Samuel. *A History of the Valley of Virginia*. 4th ed. Harrisonburg, VA: C.J. Carrier Company, 1981. Originally published 1833.

Kleece, Richard B. *Shenandoah County in the Civil War: The Turbulent Years*. Lynchburg, VA: H.E. Howard and Company, 1992.

Krick, Robert K. *Conquering the Valley: Stonewall Jackson at Port Republic*. Baton Rouge: Louisiana State University Press, 2002.

Lewis, Thomas A. *The Guns of Cedar Crook*. New York: Harper & Row Publishers, 1988.

Longacre, Edward G. *Lincoln's Cavalrymen: A History of the Mounted Forces of the Army of the Potomac*. Mechanicsburg, PA: Stackpole Books, 2000.

Mahon, Michael G. *The Shenandoah Valley, 1861–1865: The Destruction of the Granary of the Confederacy*. Mechanicsburg, PA: Stackpole Books, 1999.

Mahon, Michael G., ed. *Winchester Divided: The Civil War Diaries of Julia Chase & Laura Lee*. Mechanicsburg, PA: Stackpole Books, 2002.

McDonald, Archie P., ed. *Make Me a Map of the Valley: The Civil War Journal of Stonewall Jackson's Topographer, Jedediah Hotchkiss*. Dallas, TX, 1973.

McDonald, Cornelia Peake. *A Woman's Civil War: A Diary, with Reminiscences of the War, from March 1862*. Edited by Minrose C. Gwin. New York: Gramercy Books, 2003.

Moore, Albert B. *Conscription and Conflict in the Confederacy*. Columbia: University of South Carolina Press, 1996.

Moore, Robert H., II. *Tragedy in the Shenandoah Valley: The Story of the Summers-Koontz Execution*. Charleston, SC: The History Press, 2006.

Neil, Alexander. *Alexander Neil and the Last Shenandoah Valley Campaign: Letters of an Army Surgeon to His Family, 1864*. Shippensburg, PA: White Mane, 1996.

Official Atlas of the Civil War. New York: Thomas Yoseloff, 1968.

Painter, Fred P. *Shenandoah County and Its Courthouse*. Shenandoah County, VA, 1979.

Patchan, Scott C. *Shenandoah Summer: The 1864 Valley Campaign*. Lincoln: University of Nebraska Press, 2007.

Philips, Edward H. *The Lower Shenandoah Valley in the Civil War: The Impact of War Upon the Civilian Population and Upon Civil Institutions*. Lynchburg, VA: H.E. Howard and Company, Inc., 1993.

Robertson, James I., Jr. *Stonewall Jackson: The Man, the Soldier, the Legend*. New York: Macmillan Publishing, 1997.

Shanks, Henry T. *The Secession Movement in Virginia, 1847–1861*. Richmond, VA: Garrett and Massie, Inc., 1934.

Sheehan-Dean, Aaron. *Why Confederates Fought: Family and Nation in Civil War Virginia*. Chapel Hill: University of North Carolina Press, 2007.

Shriver, Ernest. "Stealing Railroad Engines." In *Tales from McClure's War: Being True Stores of Camp and Battlefield*. New York: Doubleday & McClure, Co., 1989.

Southern Claims Commission Master Index, 1871–1880. Guide to the Records of the U.S. House of Representatives at the National Archives, 1789–1989 (Record Group 233).

Stewart, Nancy B. "How Slavery Operated in Shenandoah County." www.shenandoahcountyhistoricalsociety.org (accessed March 11, 2012).

———. "Who Got into the Slavery Business in Shenandoah .County?" www.shenandoahcountyhistoricalsociety.org (accessed March 8, 2012).

Tanner, Robert G. *Stonewall in the Valley: Thomas J. "Stonewall" Jackson's Shenandoah Valley Campaign, Spring 1862*. Mechanicsburg, PA: Stackpole Books, 1996.

Taylor, James E. *Sketchbook and Diary*. Dayton, OH: Morningside House, Inc., 1989.

Turner, E. Raymond. *The New Market Campaign, May 1864*. Richmond, VA: Whittet and Shepperson, 1912.

Union Army. *A History of Military Affairs in the Loyal States 1861–65*. Records of the Regiments in the Union Army, Cyclopedia of Battles, Memoirs of Commanders and Soldiers. 8 vols. Madison, WI: Federal Publishing, 1908.

United States War Department. *The War of the Rebellion: A Compilation of the Official Records of the Union and Confederate Armies*. Washington, D.C.: Government Printing Office, 1880–1900.

Urwin, Gregory J.W. *Custer Victorious*. East Brunswick, NJ: Associated University Presses, Inc., 1983.

Walker, Aldace Freeman. *The Vermont Brigade in the Shenandoah Valley*. Burlington: Vermont Free Press Association, 1869.

Walker, Gary C. *Yankee Soldiers in Virginia Valleys: Hunter's Raid*. Roanoke, VA: A&W Enterprise, 1989.

Warner, Ezra J. *Generals in Gray*. Baton Rouge: Louisiana State University Press, 1988.

Wayland, John W. *A History of Shenandoah County, Virginia*. Strasburg, VA: Shenandoah Publishing House, Inc., 1927. Reprint, 1969.

————. *Stonewall Jackson's Way*. Verona, VA: McClure Printing Company, Inc., 1969.

————. *Twenty-five Chapters on the Shenandoah Valley*. Strasburg, VA: Shenandoah Publishing House, Inc., 1957.

Wert, Jeffrey D. *From Winchester to Cedar Creek: The Shenandoah Campaign of 1864*. Carlisle, PA: South Mountain Press, Inc., 1987.

Wilson, James D., and Louise E. Wilson. *Edinburg 1861 to 1865: Civil War Incidents & Anecdotes*. Woodstock, VA: American Speedy Printing Centers of Shenandoah County, 1982.

Wise, Jennings Cropper. The *Long Arm of Lee*. Richmond, VA: Owens Publishing Co., 1988.

About the Author

H al Sharpe is a retired forensic scientist and criminal investor with the United States Army who resides with his wife in Edinburg, Virginia. Sharpe has a master's degree in history from Austin Peay State University in Clarksville, Tennessee, and a master's of forensic sciences from George Washington University in Washington, D.C. As a longtime student of Civil War history, particularly in the Shenandoah Valley, Mr. Sharpe has served as a member of the board of directors for the Shenandoah County Historical Society and the Edinburg Heritage Foundation. He served as a member of the historical interpretation committee of the Shenandoah Battlefield Foundation. He is the founding commander of the Captain Jack Adams Camp of the Sons of Confederate Veterans. He is also the author of numerous articles and parts of books related to the Civil War in the Shenandoah Valley.

Visit us at
www.historypress.net